French FISHING FLIES

Patterns and Recipes for Fly Tying

Books by Dr. Jean-Paul Pequegnot

Répertoire des Mouches Artificielles Françaises
1975, 1984, Besançon

l'Art de la Pêche à la Mouche Sèche
Flammarion, Paris 1969, 1977, 1981

l'Arte della Pesca con la Mosca Secca
Sperling & Kupfer, Milano, 1985

Pêche à la Mouche en Bretagne (With P. Phélipot)
1971, Besançon

La Loue
1981, Besançon

La santé de votre enfant
Flammarion, Paris, 1983

French FISHING FLIES

Patterns and Recipes for Fly Tying

DR. JEAN-PAUL PEQUEGNOT

Translated by ROBERT A. CHINO

Introduction by DATUS PROPER

New color section compiled by
PIERRE AFFRE

Skyhorse Publishing

Skyhorse Publishing books may be purchased in bulk at special discounts for sales promotion, corporate gifts, fund-raising, or educational purposes. Special editions can also be created to specifications. For details, contact the Special Sales Department, Skyhorse Publishing, 307 West 36th Street, 11th Floor, New York, NY 10018 or info@skyhorsepublishing.com.

Visit our website at www.skyhorsepublishing.com.

10 9 8 7 6 5 4 3 2 1

Library of Congress Cataloging-in-Publication Data is available on file.

ISBN: 978-1-61608-544-5

Printed in China

Contents

Introduction 7
Preface to the English Language Edition 13
New color section follows page 64
Mouchettes of the Ain 17
Altière 19
Andelle 20
Assassine 22
Béhotière 24
Bonnenfant 26
Bourrue du Rhône 27
Chenille 29
Crème du Guiers 33
Cul de Canard 34
Diaphanoptères 36
Dindin 37
Flies of the Ellé 39
Mouches Exquises 43
Farfelue 46
Favorite of Carrère 47
Favorite of de Chamberet 48
Favorite of Gallay 49
Gallica 50
Gamma 52
Germinal 53
Gloire de Goumois 54
Gloire de Neublans 56
Grise à Corps Jaune 57
Incomparable 60
Irrésistible de Cuvelier 62
Jacotte 63
Jean-Marie 64

Nymphe Jeannot 66
Joliette 67
Lefrançois 69
Léhodey 71
Lemarchand 72
Lièvre et Perdrix 73
Loge-Coucou 75
La Loue 77
Mademoiselle Rose 79
Mistigri 81
Montréal 84
Mouche Noire de l'Odet 86
Orange et Faisan 87
Ornans 89
Pallareta 90
Palm-Ailes 91
Panama 93
Patate 96
Paysanne 97
Pébé 99
Peute 100
Phryga-Nymphe 101
Plantureuse 103
Plumeaux 105
Poil de Lièvre 106
Pont-Audemer 107
Président Billard 109
Preska 110
Professionnelle 112
Reine de Cademène 113
Ruz-Du 115
Sub-May 116
Touyllon 118
Tricolore 119
Universelle 120
Victoire 122
Viroise 124
X 125

Introduction

It is about time someone published a good book in English on the French fly-fishing tradition. We know that France is rich in most resources—natural, human, artistic, and gustatory—but how many of us have fished there? The country is not, for anglers, what the travel agents call a "destination resort." I recall one useful reference in an American book (by Leonard Wright) and none in any American magazine.

This book is mostly about flies. You might like to know something about the streams and fish too, and I can't help much. What I know comes from a few hours of fishing in France, a few days in Switzerland, and a few years in Portugal. That at least gets me through the culture shock, which, for an American of the catch-and-release generation, is considerable.

My American and British friends generally dropped out. I stayed with the fishing mainly, I guess, because a trout stream in Europe plays the same music as a trout stream in the Appalachians, and because it hurts to stay in town when the buds are breaking and the rains are washing angleworms across the sidewalks. It is also painful to watch a stream being cleaned out, whether with bait or flies or spin-bubbles. But my European friends treat me well. They also treat trout well—once they are in the creel—and I can appreciate the idea that the highest destiny of a fish is to be poached in white wine. It's sort of like the Congressional Medal of Honor, which is a splendid thing to have if you're dead anyhow.

Latin Europe convinced me that the brown trout is as good a product as nature ever got around to evolving. Those I caught were mostly small, mind you, but their freedom lent a feeling of wilderness to hills that had been populated since the last Ice Age. Each stream had its own strain, different in appearance and habits from trout in the next watershed, but having in common centuries of experience in avoiding nets and setlines and maggots and, more recently, insects that look like everyday food but have a sting to them.

You can take it that the French professionals did not persist in fly fishing for reasons aesthetic. Their income came from their catch, and, judging from this book, they found it profitable to fish small flies on or near the surface. So did I. When I could see the fly—even at a distance on fast water—I had a chance of controlling its behavior, and perhaps of hooking the only legal-sized trout of the day. It did seem important to imitate the behavior and size of the natural insects. I did not see much selectivity to color or even to shape—but then I never got on the French chalkstreams or the fertile rivers that Dr. Pequegnot fishes.

Most of the streams I tried would look comfortable to you if you knew the upper Willowemoc in New York, Big Run in Virginia, the Pecos in New Mexico, or another small freestone water with wild trout. And your American flies would work in southern Europe. By the same token, you might reckon that your fly box is getting inbred, and this book will provide healthy stock for an outcross. The flies won't look foreign to the trout in your home stream.

France—like America—has been influenced by the English fishing tradition. Dr. Pequegnot makes this clear. But in the French case, English ideas were imposed on native habits. That was not the case in English-speaking America: for us, the culture of angling began in England, was lifted intact to the New World, and then changed in response to local conditions. The change was remarkably slow; Americans still use artificial flies called Iron Blue Duns and Blue-Winged Olives, even though we lack the natural British flies on which the artificial ones were originally based.

We also retain the old concepts of patterns, in which flies—or at least serious, imitative flies—are classified by color (look again at Iron Blue and Blue-Winged Olive). If an artificial fly does not resemble the natural in color, then most of us do not consider it imitative. We may catch a trout on a fly that resembles the natural in behavior, size, and shape, but if the color is different, we conclude (by a remarkable leap of logic) that the trout was not selective.

In what category, then, shall we place a fly that happens to be "rose champagne" in color? *La Loue* is not intended to imitate a specific insect. But it is small, it is soberly dressed (for the color-blind), and it has the shape traditionally associated with representations of mayfly duns. Furthermore, it takes difficult fish—and I gather that they include trout, though it started as a grayling fly. The Halfordian solution would be to discard this creation as philosophically inconvenient. Dr. Pequegnot does not take that way out. He tries *La Loue*, finds it "neither more nor less effective" at catching fish than other hackle flies, but recommends it because of its remarkable visibility to the angler. This kind of analysis may seem brutally frank (if you have made an investment in expensive hackles of many hues), but it is not culture-bound.

For most of us, the important thing about this book is not that it is French but that it is one of the few works of any nationality on the design of trout flies. The author did not simply collect French fly patterns. If he had, he would have produced an interesting curiosity, but he would not have sent many Americans to their fly-tying vises. The best patterns evolve around local insects, and when transplanted to another environment, the patterns are often abandoned or modified—as happened with the Blue-Winged Olive, of which nothing is left (in America) except the name. *Good design, on the other hand, is universal.* That is as true of trout flies as of aircraft, furniture, and your wife's blue jeans. And design is why this book has as much to do with the Henry's Fork as with the Risle.

- By "design," I mean that Dr. Pequegnot explains each fly's structure and how it affects behavior on the water. (I never understood how the peculiar architecture of the Mole Fly was supposed to work until I read his description of the *Pont-Audemer*, a derivative dressing.)

- He appraises other fly-tiers' contributions as fairly as his own. (This gives us a wide range of alternatives from which to choose.)
- He discusses the advantages and disadvantages of each structural change, without excessive reverence for the mythology of the matter. (By this kind of analysis, he has developed the old Fore-&-Aft Fly more highly than anyone else.)
- He uses color as an element in design, but rarely as the leading element. (The male and female Panama are color variations, and you should not miss the author's comment on "fishermen *seriously* comparing the relative merits of the two sexes.")
- Most of his favorite flies share an elegant simplicity. (Check the sedges.)
- Of pretense there is none. (It is unlikely that old Simonet was trying to prove anything when tying the featured *Grise à Corps Jaune*, but he made a dry fly with one hook, one feather, and one piece of thread. I hope someone thought to carve that on his tombstone.)

Finally, Dr. Pequegnot's materials are few and natural, so that you can reproduce most of his favorite flies anywhere, any time, even if you are reading this in 2186. All this adds up to good flies—not just French flies.

The French names will send some misleading signals to English speakers. In both Britain and America, we have unwritten codes by which we can distinguish the deep-thinking flies from the frivolous. Of course, the fly shops still sell Adamses and Greenwell's Glorys, but your angler with flip-down magnifying glasses and felt soles is not sure whether he should put fancy flies in his number-one Wheatley fly box. What, then, will he make of creations called The Lout, or the Exquisite Fly, or the Assassin? Dr. Pequegnot does not claim that they are imitative flies, so I will make the claim on his behalf. These flies represent natural insects—generically but well. If those educated French trout do not agree with our concept of imitation, then we need another concept.

Dr. Pequegnot, in any case, is not to be blamed for the flies' names. He has adopted the honorable custom of giving the originator of any fly full credit for it, and then using the name that the originator chose. This is his main device for conveying information about French angling history. One could wish that the originators had settled for something in between The Lout and the Exquisite, but then France had no Halford and Marryat to establish a dry-fly code for rich men.

The French history had some surprises for me. In that connection, there is a point that should be made for the record. In my 1982 book, I described a design called the "Bent-Hackle Fly" and said it was, in my experience, about the best available representation of a Green Drake. I picked the design up in Ireland and assumed that it had originated there or in Britain. That may be correct, but Dr. Pequegnot describes something structurally identical under the name *Plumeaux*. There are other cases in which I could have learned from his writing, and will from now on.

Note to fly-tiers: I asked Dr. Pequegnot what hook scale he used for sizing his flies. He replied that the Redditch scale is the only one accepted in France and, further, that French tiers frown on the liberties taken by certain other countries with hook sizes. He may have been looking in our direction. The Mustad 94840 hook (often used here for dry flies) runs large. The Mustad 3906 hook and several Partridge models seem to follow Redditch sizes.

Datus C. Proper

Preface to the English Language Edition

The French fell under the spell of fly fishing much later than the English. Their literature on this subject is both younger and less prolific than that of the Anglo-Saxons. Yet, the image of great numbers of fishermen peacefully dabbling their lines along the banks of the Seine is indelibly graven into the memories of all tourists who come to Paris. There is no doubt that the French are people who love fishing—at least one out of every ten Frenchmen is a passionate fisherman.

The delay of the French in coming to the most elegant and elaborate form of angling has been attributed by some to sociological reasons. Prior to the French Revolution, the right to fish was reserved almost exclusively for the nobility or certain religious communities. They, in turn, leased these rights to some professional fishers who used nets or fish-snares. Even in salmon and trout rivers, these rare and costly creatures were seldom taken on hooks and lines. The lords preferred hunting, a right that was also reserved for them. Some historians believe it was precisely these restrictions, very frustrating for the majority of the population, that contributed not only to the start of the revolution but also to its ultimate success in the countryside. Be that as it may, the accomplished revolution permitted the common people to fish. And this gift was not withdrawn during the subsequent restoration of the monarchy. The revolution took place in 1789, and in the years that followed, the development of angling was extraordinary. In the nineteenth century, fly fishing emerged suddenly from nothing, or perhaps developed quickly from some very primitive methods that might always have existed in the shadows.

During the first half of the nineteenth century the French fished with flies using long two-handed rods made of roseau, a swamp cane. Then English materials and methods were imported from across the channel. The use of one-handed rods made of exotic wood, called "English Rods," steadily replaced the more rustic local equipment.

But the development of fly fishing in France was not destined to be only a simple imitation of that which already existed in England. Many of the newcomers to this most handsome art proved to have a certain native creativity that imparted a character to the French school, most notably in the flies themselves.

It is important to note that France is a country rich in various types of salmonid rivers. The climate is predominantly Atlantic in influence and precipitation is relatively high. There are many mountain formations that produce splendid trout rivers. The plains are often calciferous. The vast Parisian basin includes a goodly number of characteristic chalkstreams with waters of high quality. The Seine itself, in its upper reaches, is one of the most handsome chalkstreams in the world.

This magnificent domain has always been abused by destructive fishing methods. But it is certain that, for the Frenchmen who had the good taste to fish with flies at the end of the nineteenth and beginning of the twentieth centuries, there was a sort of golden age. They enjoyed astonishing catches of splendid wild fish.

Flies of all types were used. English models, preferred by the city dwellers, were either imported or simply imitated. Others, invented by inspired amateurs, tended to resemble English conceptions. Whether imitative of nature or generic, they were developed, often elaborately, to be more sophisticated than the English designs. The *Gallica* series, on one hand, or the *Panama* fly on the other, are good examples of this trend. But they seem to have created no interest for English anglers.

Of much more interest are flies of the professional fishers of France. The existence of professional fly anglers is one of the unique things about the history of fly fishing here during the first half of the twentieth century. These fishers lived partially, or entirely, by their fly rods. Taking advantage of the lack of regulations, they sold trout to the well-to-do of the villages and to restaurants. This abusive practice was ended, for the most part, with the development of trout farms producing rainbow trout for the market, and also because of the law of 1961 that prohibited sale of wild salmonids. But, until then, the professionals were fishermen of great skill, who, for obvious reasons of economy, tied their own flies. These were generally quite simple so that they could be tied rapidly and stand up under hard use. The bodies were never complicated and consisted, generally, of only one or two layers of tying thread. The flies never had wings. But the quality of their hackle was sometimes remarkable for the simple reason that the length of float and durability of a fly depends directly upon the quality of the hackle used.

Let us stop for a moment to consider hackle. An unlimited passion for really top quality hackle is a characteristic of French fly fishers. This obsession is very highly developed in the Limousin region where many fly fishermen of the countryside have one or more "fishing cocks," precious animals that furnish the rare natural gray hackle (blue dun), and that are never killed. For a French amateur, the idea of sacrificing a good cock in order to harvest the hackle is inconceivable. This would be like killing a bird that produces feathers of gold. Some of the animals cost a veritable fortune. And the cost of their freshly plucked hackle makes the price of an entire American cape, at sixty-five dollars, seem very cheap indeed. Between French fly fishermen, there is no gift more appreciated than a few really exceptional hackles.

Finally then, the lesson of effectiveness learned from the professional fishermen—presentation of the fly and leader on the water—is another characteristic of the French school. In general, and even more so for the author of these lines, the French fly fishers are more "presentationists" than "imitationists." To take their brown trout, which are perhaps the most difficult in the world, the French are more concerned with how a fly is presented than with the Anglo-Saxon concept of "matching the hatch." They use abstract patterns that can be said to be fancy and not imitative.

Very skillful fishermen, the French and their close cousins, the Belgians and the Swiss, do not have much feeling for conservation or, at least, not conservation on the same level as their fishing skill. As a result the rivers are devastated. But I believe confidence can be placed in the effectiveness of their flies.

These pages contain some of the flies that bear French names and are described in French fishing literature or sold in France. I have included some francophonic flies from Belgium, Switzerland, and even of Quebec, since all these creations have come from kindred spirits belonging to the same culture. I hope they will contribute an original note to the common patrimony of all fly fishers.

I would like to acknowledge with gratitude the efforts of all those who have assisted in the preparation of an English language edition of my little work. First of all, Robert A. Chino, one of my American fishing companions, who is responsible for the translation from my native language to his. Then Datus C. Proper, who so generously gave of his time and original knowledge of fly design to ensure that my French conceptions would be perfectly communicated to English language readers. And finally to a host of others whose help is equally appreciated.

J. P. Pequegnot
Besançon, France

JEAN-PAUL PEQUEGNOT

Mouchettes of the Ain

(Little Flies of the Ain River)

Charles de Massas, who lived in Lyon from 1827 to 1829, described fly fishing for grayling as was then practiced on the river Ain. It was done with little flies on horsehair snells made up into casts of seven or eight flies and fished on braided horsehair lines. These little flies were dressed on what de Massas called "needle hooks" because they were made from sewing needles that had been softened, bent into shape, and then retempered. This process gave them a distinctive whitish color.

The local fishermen did not have reels at that time, so they waded the waters and the many grayling and little trout they caught were played by hand manipulation of the lines. But, as de Massas pointed out, this method did not allow conquest of the larger trout, which regularly escaped.

The years have passed. For a long time, the Ain anglers continued to use old equipment that had come down to them from a distant past: long two-handed rods of nineteen to twenty feet in length, braided horsehair lines, and casts of six to ten little grayling flies called *mouchettes*. Fishing reels came into use only between the two World Wars. Prior to that time, many grayling fishermen attached a length of elastic between the rod tip and line, a predecessor of the *Roubaisian* elastic that is still used by bait fishermen in the coarse fishing contests that are a unique element of the French fishing scene.

Louis Rouquet, a judge of Poncin, described the Ain fishing of the beginning of this century. His interesting articles, which appeared in the *Chasseur Français*, have been brought together in a book entitled *Au bord de l'Eau*. Even so, we are in the process of forgetting this original and magnificent school of angling that once existed in France.

A hundred years after Charles de Massas, L. de Boisset (Léonce Vallette), in some agreeable pages, called our attention to the famous little flies of the Ain and those great anglers of Pont d'Ain, Beau and Roussillier, who tied and sold these flies and who, above all, used them with so much talent.

The *mouchettes* were tied on reversed white hooks of fine wire, with long and narrow eyeless tips, called "Italian hooks," in sizes 10 to 14. A horsehair and piece of Japanese gut was tied on the hook, then the body was made of various colored silks, ribbed with tinsel, and varnished. They were then finished with a few turns of soft hackle at the head, often trimmed, and sometimes had tails.

These little flies were fished across or diagonally downstream, wet or, more often, semi-wet or "moist." Today they are still to be seen on the Ain and can be found in local fishing tackle stores mounted with nylon of about $^{18}/_{100}$ centimeters (.007 inch).

Alas, mourn the shades of de Massas, Rouquet, Beau and Roussillier! The great two-handed rods have disappeared, replaced by the sad "Castabubbles." The celebrated casts are used only with spinning reels. The diesel motor has killed off the great sailing barges. The aesthetic loss is inestimable, for nothing was more handsome than fly fishing with those two-handed rods—the movements were large and majestic, but graceful. Splendid indeed.

Altière

The Altier is one of the best rivers of the Cévennes. In its lower parts it contains good but difficult trout that often feed on little Diptera. Raymond Rocher takes them with the fly he has named after his favorite river, and which he has described in his book, *Confidences d'un Pêcheur à la Mouche.*

Hook:	16 to 20, short shank, fine wire
Body:	Fibers of an exotic bird, the Numidie, which came from Mauritania, or lacking that, pheasant tail fibers
Hackle:	A very small black cock hackle
Wings:	Two medium-gray cock hackle tips laid back over the body and longer than the shank

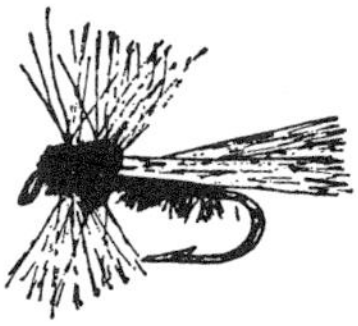

(Drawing—Serge Pestel)

The Numidie bird is a rare type of vulture found only in northwestern Africa. Aimé Devaux used its feathers to dress this fly as number 428 of his series. Raymond Rocher satisfies himself with a dark pheasant tail fiber.

The *Altière* suggests any of a multitude of little Diptera, which Rocher calls *minimoucherons*, and it also well represents winged ants.

In the immense literature of English fishing, each author has, for the Diptera, his personal variant of the Black Gnat. This French version is certainly as good. Its drawbacks are the fragility of the body and its poor visibility, which is a problem with all the little dark flies.

Andelle

Around 1946–47, André Ragot, along with some anglers of Rouen and Gisors, experimented on the Lévrière and Andelle rivers with large mayfly nymphs. Two patterns proved to be very effective and were given the names of these two Norman chalkstreams. Since then, they have been made by Ragot and sold by all the fishing-tackle dealers of Paris.

These two heavily dressed and unweighted models represent nymphs about to transform themselves into subimagos and are fished in or just under the surface film. Their clever and original dressings consist of duck hackle tied in at the head and then bent back to cover the hook shank, which is thus completely hidden. The hackle is then tied off at the hook bend.

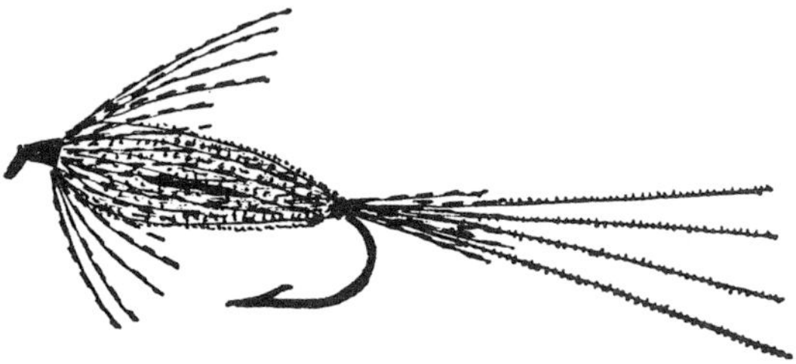

(Drawing—Serge Pestel)

Here is the design for the *Andelle.*

Hook:	8 to 10
Body:	Any color of wool covered by the fibers of a gray mallard feather tied in at the head, bent back, and tied off at the hook bend with a few turns of yellow thread
Tails:	Three or four pheasant tail fibers
Hackle:	French partridge hackle dyed yellow with picric acid

The *Lévrière* differs from the *Andelle* only in the color of the duck feather, here beige, and by replacement of the French partridge hackle by one of grouse.

Many English authors, starting with G. E. M. Skues, the father of nymph fishing, consider the usefulness of the nymph doubtful at the moment of the emergence of *E. danica*. My own experience, and that of many French anglers, is quite firm. It is effective and often essential to use a nymphal representation to tempt certain large trout where nymphs are emerging from sandy-muddy bottoms.

Recently, Serge Pestel developed a number of weighted patterns based on the *Andelle* for use on big rainbow trout of lakes and reservoirs. These variants are tied in different colors, either on simple long-shank hooks in size 10, or on a tandem of hooks with an 8 at the front and a 10 at the rear. In order to allow the lure to dip when the line is relaxed, a laquered lead bead decorated with a yellow eye is fixed at the head. This fly has a fearsome effect in running waters, and not only on trout. Like the original *Andelle*, the variants are sold by the Ragot company.

Assassine

With this fly, I wanted to combine the advantages of the high-floating palmer with the indisputable attraction of speckled partridge hackle. This hackle probably reminds fish of the joints of insect appendages. From the first experiments with this model in 1964, the number of its victims has been such that the name seems logical. Since then, the effectiveness of the *Assassine* has confirmed this impression and I find it to be by far the most killing of my flies.

Hook: 10 to 14
Tails: None
Body: Yellow tying silk

At the head, two turns of gray or brown French partridge hackle that is well speckled, and along the body a single long and natural gray cock hackle, palmered.

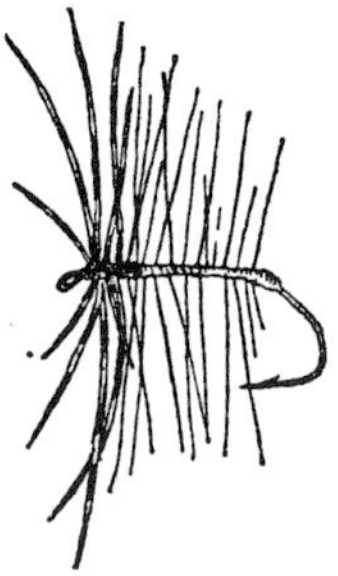

While this is a simple enough fly to dress, some care is required. The partridge hackle, significantly longer than the body hackle, should be wound first with the concave (dull) side facing forward in such a manner that, once tied in, it points a little toward the front and resists bending backward with use. The cock hackle is then wound, with a few turns, rather tightly up against the partridge hackle to provide a support. The remaining turns are then spaced out along the body to give a ringed appearance. The finishing knot is made at the rear, on the bend of the hook. If a tail is desired, the tip of the cock hackle can be left without trimming.

The only difficulty with this fly is the fragility of the partridge hackle. It is necessary to use a light touch in winding the tips of the little partridge feathers when a smaller than size 14 fly is required.

I use the *Assassine* in a large size—10—mostly during the hatch of the Green Drake, and I owe many of my large wild French trout to it. Still, the *Assassine* does not pretend to represent any particular insect or group of insects. It is a fly of abstract design whose effectiveness seems to show that there is a place for artificials that strive for specific qualities and take off on flights of imagination, as well.

Béhotière

This was the name of the country house of Edouard Vernes at Valleville on the banks of the Risle. Charles Ritz tells us that the fishing of Valleville was better than that of any other chalk-stream in Europe.

The *Béhotière*, one of the preferred flies of Edouard Vernes, was created for him by Ogareff. It is a curious mixture of a mayfly and a sedge.

Hook:	10 to 12, black tying silk
Tails:	Spotted mallard duck fibers
Body:	Green wool
Hackle:	Reddish brown, at the head
Wings:	Two, laid back at the rear, of grizzly hackle points

In effect, the body and wings strongly suggest the sedge, and the tails a mayfly. Everything necessary is here to shock an entomologist—and also to take a good trout.

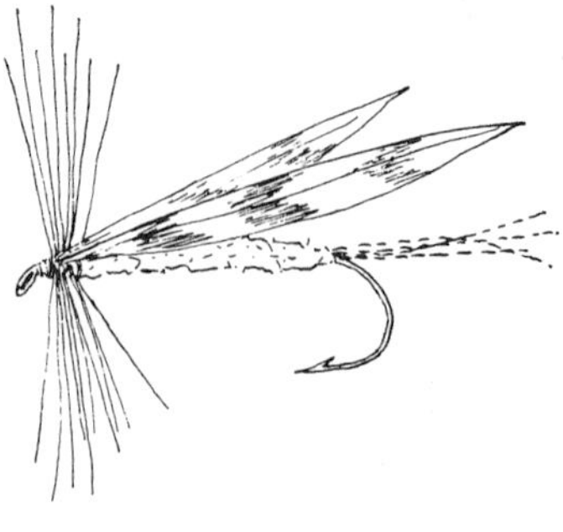

Bonnenfant

The famous salmon fisher, Lucien Bonnenfant, used flies in which the general structure was like British models, but whose wings were partially or totally replaced by a pinch of badger hair.

Badger, donkey, or mule hair has been popular for a long time along the banks of the Allier, where Bonnenfant carried out most of his exploits. Today the British use tube flies for salmon fishing, plastic tubes furnished with a cone of hair and armed with triple hooks. While I must deplore, in passing, the use of such inelegant things as treble hooks for fly fishing, I admit that, in general, fur has a greater attraction for salmon than feathers. This is no reason for regret because flies can be quite as handsome when made with fur as with feathers. This superiority of hair is not limited to salmon. It seems to me that it is equally good with nymphs and wet flies for trout.

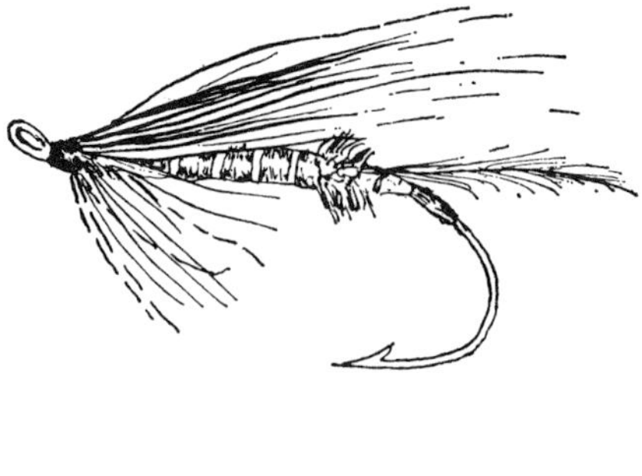

Bourrue du Rhône

(Lout of the Rhône)

L. de Boisset loved fishing for the grayling of the river Rhône, especially during autumn. He used wet flies and fished around Pont de Lucey up to Culoz. It pleased him to say that the more a fly has a loutish and rumpled appearance, the better it fishes. A simple palmer with mediocre reddish brown hackle wound on 12 to 16 hooks, a few scissor slices to trim the hackle close to the shank all along its length except for a little collar at the head, and some tails was the fly he loved and called the *Bourrue du Rhône.*

It is likely that this fly was created around 1936 or 1937, but de Boisset never mentioned it in any of his books. Without a doubt the reason for this omission is to be found in the contradiction of this fly to his stated imitationist philosophy. It is, nonetheless, still used in the region of Lyon and is sold in Lyon itself in the store of Pierre Bourret.

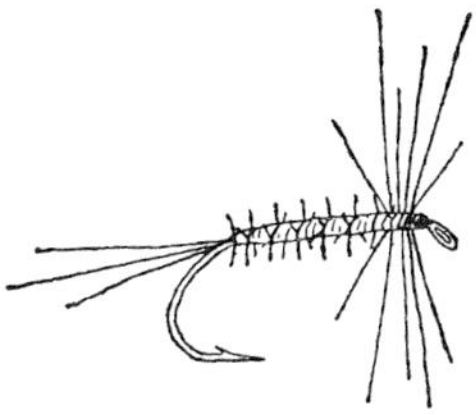

Trimming the hackles results in a very lively and attractive body. It is simple to dress, not only for wet flies and nymphs, but even more so for dry flies. The process could be expanded and generalized with brilliant results. In this spirit, I have created a variant of the *Grise à Corps Jaune* which, acknowledging the origin of the idea, I have named *Bourrue du Doubs*, because I first used it on the river Doubs. It is particularly indicated in the presence on the water of *Baetis rhodani*, but it is also a good general-purpose fly. It is tied as follows:

Hook:	12 to 16
Tails:	Gray spade hackle fibers or, if possible, pardo spade hackle fibers
Body:	Yellow tying silk ribbed with a dark gray hackle (trimmed)
Hackle:	Gray head hackle

An explanation of the pardo hackle is given with the fly *Incomparable.* To be sure, the trimmed body hackle can be mediocre, but the head hackle should be of the best possible quality.

Chenille

I use this term rather than the English equivalent *palmer*, not to diminish the large part the English have played in the development of the art of fly fishing, but as homage to Charles de Massas, the first good French fishing author. His charming and enthusiastic little book, *Le Pêcheur à la mouche artificielle*, went through several editions in the course of the last century and was an important factor in the increased popularity of fly fishing in France.

De Massas had a strong personality and a splendid absence of prejudice. He was acquainted with the English style of fly fishing, already well developed in the first half of the nineteenth century, but judged the necessary equipment to be too sophisticated, too fragile, and above all, too expensive. He perfected rustic material that was easily made by the handymen of our country and that mainly consisted of a long reed two-

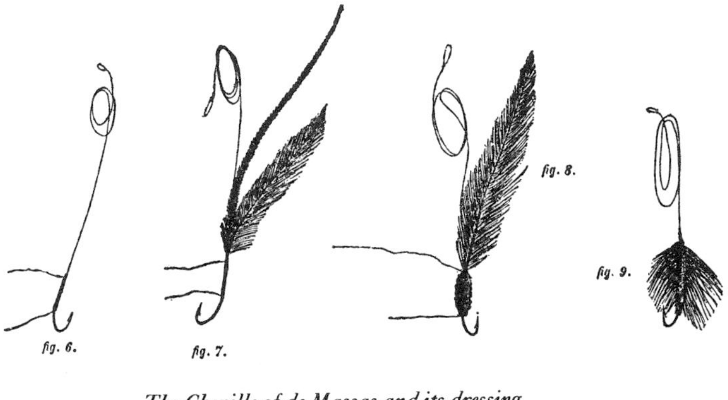

The Chenille of de Massas and its dressing

handed rod, a simple reel, a "string" line impregnated with drying oil, and two fly patterns. In fact, he considered that only one of these two patterns, with its two wings, could be considered worthy of being called a fly. The other, the one he preferred, simply had the name of *Chenille*. This fly had a body of peacock or ostrich with a single cock hackle tied in at the head and wound back all along the body. De Massas gave no importance to color. He barely admitted that it was better to use dark or light colors under certain circumstances of weather or water. He was satisfied simply to vary the size of his *Chenilles*.

De Massas was certainly not the inventor of this dressing. It is found in the engravings of more ancient flies and probably is as old as fly fishing itself, with origins that are lost in the past.

Contrary to what has been written by certain authors who fix the origin of the dry fly in the last quarter of the nineteenth century with Marryat and Halford, it seems certain that Charles de Massas, and probably his predecessors and disciples, used the *Chenille* as a dry fly. The principal quality of bushy artificials is their stubborn float that is evident even when the quality of hackle is doubtful and drying by false casting is less than perfect. De Massas makes this quite explicit when he recommends preventing the line from sinking so that "it will not drown the fly," and keeping the fly "on the surface of the water," and avoiding using heavy hooks to prevent the sinking of the fly.

After de Massas, the penetration in France of English fishing literature and the success of the book by G. Albert Petit, all of which were devoted to the imitationism of Halford, pushed the *Chenille* into obscurity. It was, after all, representative of nothing and certainly not of the Ephemeroptera, then considered to be the only important family of insects worthy of imitation by fly dressers. Almost all "educated" anglers saw it as a secondary pattern and, often, as a fly to be used only for chub.

However, in 1932 the palmer reappeared in the *Tricolore*, a pattern André Ragot proposed as a general fly. But it still had a little body towards the bend as well as tails, those sacred tails

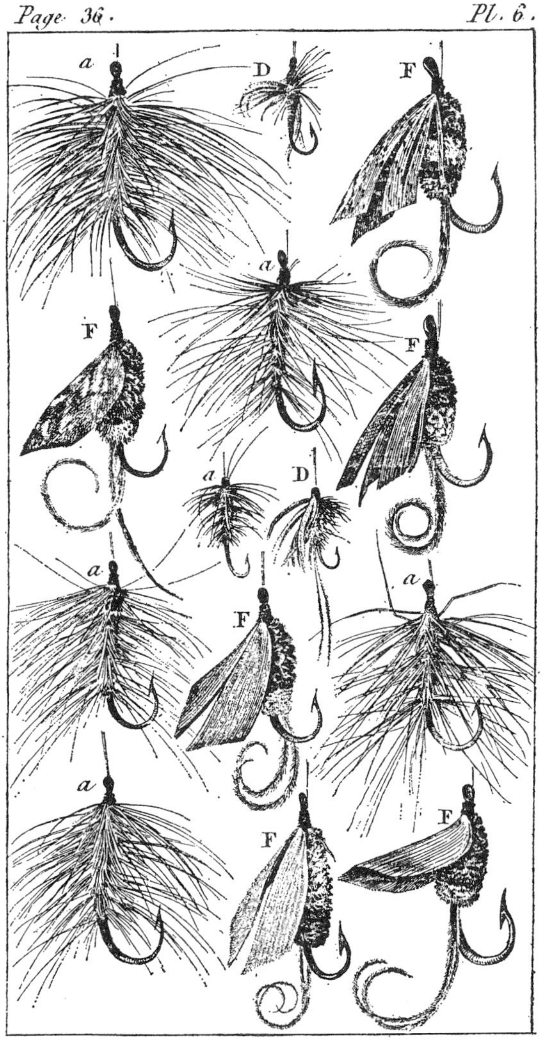

Engraving from the "Pêcheur Français" of Kresz Ainé, 1818
The flies marked F *are given by Kresz as flies for carp*

that please the angler so much and that cause so many missed strikes.

It was inevitable that a fisherman would eliminate these nonessential details and return to the basic *Chenille*. Henri Bresson, a formidable taker of trout, wanted a fly that would float very high and be effective under almost all conditions for trout and grayling. He needed this because part of his livelihood came from his fishing rod. Without doubt, he wanted an original pattern and one that could be sold. Not having any idea of its antecedents, he reinvented the *Chenille*, adding a little diversity to its silhouette. He placed three hackles of different colors, one after the other, along the body, which was made up of three different colors of tying thread. He baptised his fly the *French Tricolore*, a name that did not bring any pleasure to André Ragot. And Bresson, not knowing any English, did not hesitate to mix English and French spellings.

This *Tricolore*, like the others, was successful with fly fishermen. Having used a goodly number of variations of my own development, I am sure of its superiority over more classic forms of floating flies, an advantage even more pronounced when one has to deal with very difficult trout. It is an error to believe that *Chenilles* are flies that are good only for swift mountain streams. They prove themselves brilliantly on the slow waters of chalkstreams despite the antipathy toward them of fishermen who are habituated to these calm waters.

This attitude is, in my opinion, due to the much less agreeable aspect of the *Chenille* when compared to a pretty fly with well-dressed wings. In addition, this type of fly brings to our art a note of simplicity not to the taste of all anglers.

But it is necessary to respect the facts whether or not they are pleasing, and the fact here is that the consistent effectiveness of this most simple and ancient pattern of all known flies has been amply proven.

Crème du Guiers

For some fifty-odd years, along the banks of the river Guiers a fly has been used, although its inventor is unknown. It has no cream, other than in its name:

Hook:	12 to 14
Tails:	Reddish brown with black tips
Body:	Brown tying silk
Hackle:	Very light gray
Wings:	Reddish brown hackle with black tips tied in at an angle of ninety degrees from each other

The demand for this fly is very large in the region of Lyon, and Pierre Bourret has them made for his store by Aimé Devaux. It carries the number 879 in the Devaux collection.

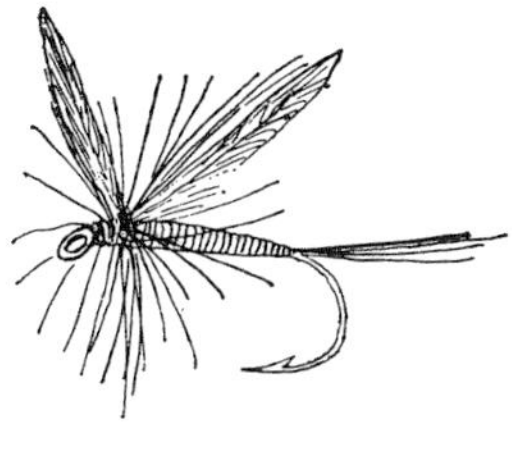

Cul de Canard

(Duck's Rump)

On most birds, a "preen gland," the uropygial gland, is found at the base of the tail feathers. It usually secretes an oily fluid the bird uses in preening its feathers. In the wild duck this gland is surrounded by some dozens of downy feathers that are somewhat wider and shorter than hackles but that can be wound on hooks. The fibers are rather too long and must be trimmed, but they result in a fly of surprising lightness that floats better than any other made of hair or feathers so long as it is not drowned, for then it is very difficult to dry. This is a very serious defect, but is of minor importance when compared to this fly's superior attraction for trout and grayling.

This unique fly was originated in Vallorbe in the Swiss section of the Jura. In Franche-Comté, where it is well known and widely used, it is sometimes called the *Mouche de Vallorbe* or, more often, the *Cul de Canard.*

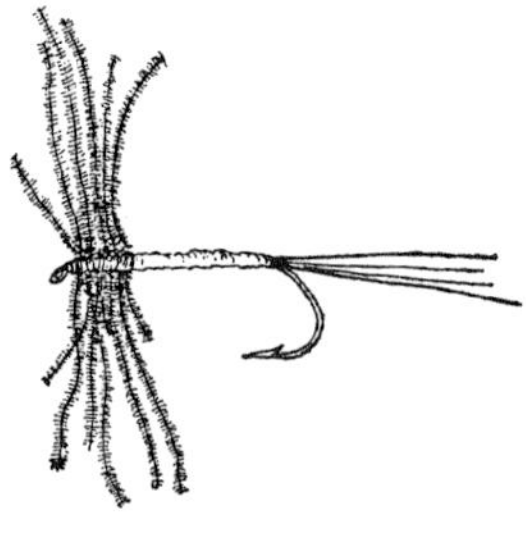

Aimé Devaux made excellent ones with a body of yellow tying silk in the Franche-Comté manner with a gray supporting hackle just behind the duck-down collar, which greatly improves the posture of the fly. He has also perfected an entire series of flies in which the head hackle is duck down and the wings are cock-hackle points. Bresson satisfied himself with duck down and his *Cul de Canard* has its fibers slanted back a little, like his *Peute*. They do not have tails.

My personal preference is for a head hackle of duck down supported by a gray cock hackle palmered in the fashion of my *Assassine*.

It is good to have this fly with you. Even if it is not used much for fear of having it definitively soaked by some little fingerling trout, it is useful in coming to terms with very difficult fish, especially grayling.

Some American readers know the name of my friend, Pierre Affre. His passion for fish and his talent was the subject of some pages in William Humphrey's story, "Cast and Cast Again." Pierre is a partisan of the *Cul de Canard*, with which he performed miracles on some of the American catch-and-release waters. It seems that some of the large trout of the Henry's Fork still have sore mouths from his passing through.

Diaphanoptères

Doctor Juge, the father of the *Mouches Exquises*, after having taken thousands of trout over thirty years with the most unrealistic flies imaginable, returned, at the end of his career, to a search for flies of greater resemblance to real insects. He abandoned one extreme for the other and came up with patterns he described in his book, *Pêcheur de Truites*, as exact imitations.

These copies of Ephemeroptera are tied on very small hooks —18 to 22 for most and 14 to 16 for the large ones. They have detached bodies and wings in plastic sheets that have been cut to form. The resemblance to living insects is very great for humans and probably for trout as well, since they rise to these false mayflys.

But these flies, sold under the name *Diaphanoptères*, did not have the sensational success that might have been expected. The reason for this is very simple: their wings are relatively stiff and instantly twist the fine tippets required for such small hooks. A twisted leader is beyond use, falling without precision and lightness in a tangle and, if by some miracle a trout takes the fly, a break-off is almost a certainty. To use such flies requires a long rod with slow action and, above all, gentle casts of only short distances. That is very difficult today with the current tendency toward short rods with fast actions. Add to that the fact that a trout hooked on a number 22 has much more chance of opening the hook. To minimize this possibility it would be necessary to use a very soft rod of a type no longer made by present-day builders. These drawbacks tend to demonstrate that resemblance to natural models is not everything in a fly and may not be even the essential factor.

Dindin

Quite some time ago the Americans, followed by the English, perfected fly lures to fish for large trout with fly rods. These fly lures are quite bulky and are cast diagonally downstream to be worked in the current in much the same manner as are salmon flies. These lures are called streamers if they are mounted with feathers, or bucktails if mounted with hair. They are generally dressed on hooks in sizes 6 to 10. In England they are used currently for large rainbow trout in artificial bodies of water where fee fisheries have been established. On these waters only the use of artificial flies is usually authorized.

For a long time, in France nothing similar was used for the sad reason that worms and minnows were widely used to take large trout. Very few anglers were interested in fishing for these really big fish with fly rods. Jean-Michel Dubos, for whom nothing to do with fly fishing was foreign, was one of the very few who were interested in trying streamers.

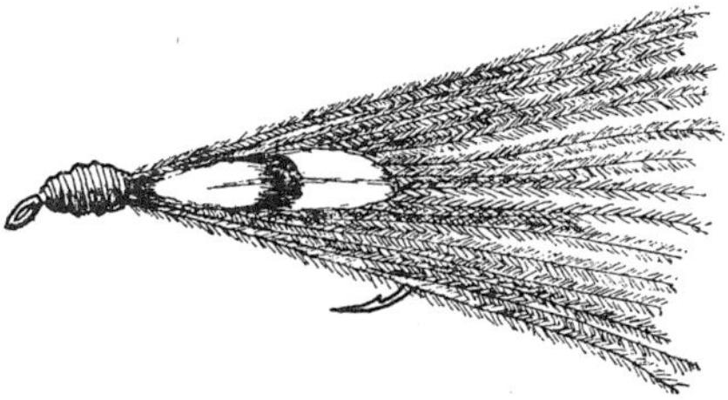

There is no point in saying that his *Dindin* was the result of a joke—the first one was made from an old feather duster. For my part, I see in it the deliberate creation of a fly lure made from attractive material with barbules of ostrich feathers.

The dressing of this fly is very simple: on a size 8 hook with a very long shank, weighted with two windings of silvered copper wire, some barbules of ostrich are tied in at the head and, if desired, shoulders of jungle cock or something similar can be added. It is finished with a large red head made of tying silk.

In the water, worked intelligently, this feather duster starts to live, weaving a little like a small squid. It should be used in the morning or the evening where one has some reason to believe that the artists of the minnow-spinner rig have perhaps overlooked a large trout.

JEAN-PAUL PEQUEGNOT

Flies of the Ellé

There have been almost no original French salmon flies for a number of reasons: a lack of sufficient salmon streams of interest for fly fishing as well as the lack of long tradition in this magnificent sport. The tens or perhaps hundreds of enthusiastic anglers who have held the big rods on the Gave or Allier have, more often than not, used British flies. These are sumptuous and poetic but complicated, and use the feathers of the rarest birds that were carried from the most distant parts of the Victorian empire.

Despite that, in Brittany there was a time when the salmon fly was widely and very well used by local anglers. This, of course, was before the modern dark ages of the spinning reel and packet of worms. The Bretons, being often country dwellers of limited financial means, did not have jungle cock or other exotic birds at their disposal. And, to be sure, the English flies did not overly impress them. With the means they had at hand, as much gumption as was required, and a little imagination, they produced sober and light flies that were appreciably different from the English flies. And their native flies proved to be quite as effective in their hands. Each had his special fly and the local champion jealously guarded his secret. There was no sign of that desire the English have of naming and defining patterns for intellectual comfort and commercialization. It was only on the Ellé, the most beautiful and best salmon river of Brittany, that a fly was developed and described enough to be called a fly of the Ellé. Two anglers of great local reputation, Francois le Ny and Henry Clerc, made a decisive contribution and it is appropriate to give here the essence of their ideas.

Francois le Ny was born in 1905 near Le Faouet and died in Quimperlé in 1963 at the end of a life as a professional fisherman of trout and salmon. He learned fly fishing from a salmon-fishing uncle and never used any other method. He was a good trout fisherman. He knew his rivers very well and knew the habits of trout. He furnished the restaurants of the region with fish. But, above all, he was an astonishing salmon angler who was equal to any test. He took at least forty-five to fifty salmon every year, more in the good years, from the public beats of the Ellé and Scorff. People still talk of the prayer book in which he carried his collection of feathers for streamside fly dressing. Unlike many famous fishermen, he freely shared his flies with others, but never sold them.

Their pattern was relatively standardized: a tail of golden pheasant tippet; a tag of red, yellow, or green wool or cotton; a heavily dressed body in boar hair that has been dyed a bronzed green with picric acid and ribbed with an ash gray cock hackle in palmer style. Silver tinsel was used only on big flies for the beginning of the season. Wings in fibers of pea hen feathers tied in the Spanish style—that is, in a fan as for a trout wet fly.

The principal characteristic of these flies was the use of local but original material, such as wild-boar hair that had been gathered by scraping the hide of animals with a fork, or pea hen feathers, which, with their handsome spotting and suppleness, impart much life to the fly in the water.

Palmered body hackle is also found in many of the Breton flies, as well as the dressing of wings in fibers rather than in entire feathers. The result, above all in the water, is the impression of great lightness. Color, reduced to a spot in the tag and tail, was not used as an element of any importance.

There is absolutely no reason to consider these flies as models of only local interest. They have proven themselves almost everywhere, in Ireland, Scotland, and Finland, especially in the hands of André Ragot, who has commercialized some versions after having fished much with Le Ny himself.

The most interesting and elaborate of the Ellé flies were those made by a clockmaker of le Pouldu, Henry Clerc, who was also born in 1905, at Morteau, in the Doubs. Today he is one of the best salmon fly fishermen in Brittany. This Franc-

Comtois, a Breton by adoption, started by fishing for trout with flies in 1928 on the Ellé and Scorff. He fished only for trout up to around 1955 when he started salmon fishing after taking his first on a trout wet fly. During that period, the grand migrator started to become much more scarce than in preceding years. But Henry Clerc still succeeded regularly, even taking five magnificent salmon at the dam of Gorrets in April 1970. His flies are the fruit of long reflection on how to improve the flies of Le Ny. The two men knew each other well, sometimes fished together, and had a mutual esteem for their flies as well as their fishing talents. Le Ny frequently declared that the flies of Clerc were better than his.

Clerc's formula is relatively simple, but it is dressed with meticulous care under a clockmaker's magnifying glass:

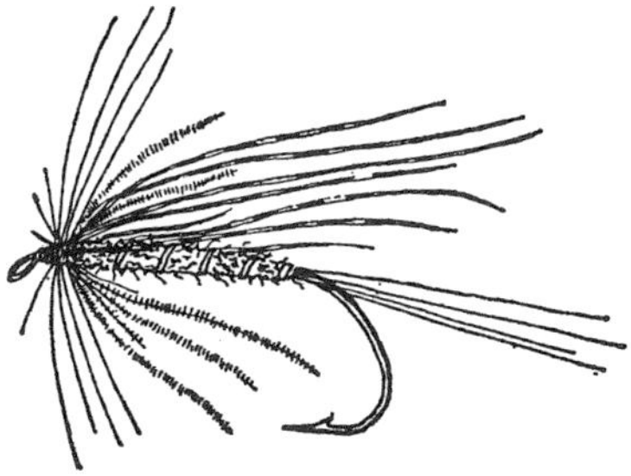

Hook:	3 to 7, brown tying silk
Tail:	Reddish-brown, no colored tag
Body:	Thin body of bronze wild-boar hair ribbed with a silver tinsel
Hackle:	Two turns of ash gray natural cock hackle wound collar-style at the head only
Wings:	Dressed in the Spanish style, in pea hen fibers with a little bunch of downy fibers at each side

This fly, in which all live color is banished, is sober, light, and transparent. It is one of the rare salmon patterns that gives the impression of a fly and not a hummingbird. Henry Clerc thinks that it is important for a hackle fly to have somewhat stiff fibers along with very supple ones, and he takes a great deal of care with judicious mixtures. This is a concern found in all the best wet-fly dressers of Brittany.

These little flies, formulated by a tier whose orientation was that of a trout fisherman, sink but a little under the surface. Clerc always fishes with a tactic close to that of the greased line of the English. He does not hesitate to fish directly across and even upstream when the configuration of the stream so requires. This is almost nymph fishing in the style of Skues.

It is upsetting that the present-day organization of salmon fishing in Brittany is not worthy of the talents of some of the fly fishermen of that beautiful region.

Mouches Exquises

(Exquisite Flies)

Doctor Juge was a country doctor in Chamberet in the Corrèze. He published a book, *Pêcheur de Truites*, in 1959, and it is in this book that we find the double-hackle collared flies that bear the charming name of *Mouches Exquises*. The author states that he conceived of this dressing in 1918 and used it almost exclusively for thirty-odd years.

Horace Brown, a fisherman of the Kennet in England, a chalkstream of great reputation, has also described a double-hackle fly called, "Fore and After" or "Fore and Aft." It seems almost certain that the two authors, English and French, did not know about each other and it is impossible to determine who came up with this idea first.

These *Mouches Exquises* have a body of tying silk and two hackle collars of equal size. One is at the rear, at the bend of the hook, and the other in its usual place, at the head. Between the two collars there is a clearly defined space. There are never tails, wings, or elaborate bodies. The general silhouette is that of an axle with two feather wheels. This silhouette is deliberately nonimitative. It might suggest the body of an ant or the coupling of a pair of some unknown Diptera. Without any doubt it represents the summit of abstractionism and is located at the other extreme from the imitationism of Halford, Skues, and de Boisset. That is certainly the reason that fishermen are even more skeptical of the *Mouches Exquises* than they are of palmers. To admit that such patterns could be effective would be to consider a goodly number of traditional truths as mere prejudices. And for many, such admission is impossible.

I first tried a double-collar fly after having read the curious book of Doctor Juge. The advantages of such a fly were quickly revealed. Float and visibility were better than for a palmer and it had a lighter and more transparent silhouette. There was less of a tendency for the hackle to lay back along the bodies after some use.

So for some twenty years I have taken more than half of my trout and grayling with these flies, giving up their use only in the presence of an abundant hatch of mayflies, sedges, or stoneflies, insects with such peculiar silhouettes that it can be amusing to try to imitate them. I have made a few disciples among my friends, but, in the final analysis, feel a certain solitude, since none of them uses the double-collared flies as much as I do.

I think that I have made a little improvement in these flies by always using a longer hackle at the head than at the tail. In this manner, it is almost certain that the tippet of the leader will form a small bridge or "swan's neck" of about 10 centimeters over the water. I firmly believe in this presentation because it avoids the deformation caused by surface tension when the leader tippet is lying on the water. It seems to me that the majority of refusals of dry flies are not due to the fly itself but to the presence of the leader tippet on the water.

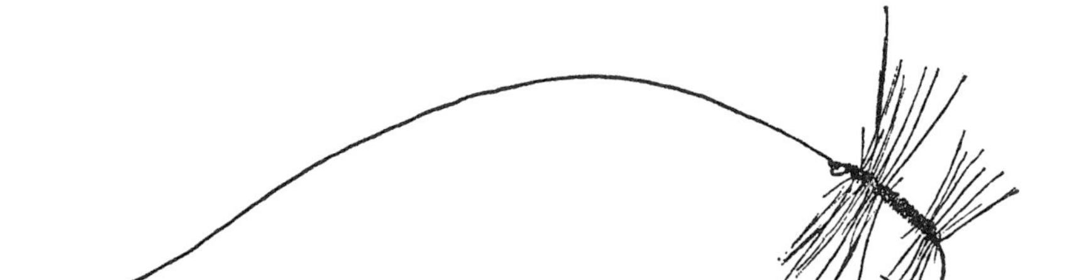

I also have a certain preference for hackle with black centers —furnace, coch-y-bondhu, badger, and honey dun—which add a contrast seemingly attractive to fish.

Here are my preferred versions of the *Mouches Exquises*, all on 12 to 18 hooks:

Coquine:	Yellow body, badger, grizzly or gray hackles. In effect, the *Grise à Corps Jaune* with a double collar
Taquine:	Red body, gray hackles
Pont-Aven:	Red body, coch-y-bondhu hackles
Gauloise Bleue:	Yellow body, dark blue-gray hackles such as those provided by the Gauloise Bleue race of cocks. This is my favorite fly and I think that I have taken several thousand fish with it

In tying in the hackles, care must be taken that the two shiny sides face each other. In this manner the two collars bend back slightly from each other and give a good seat to the fly.

Guy Plas, the celebrated hackle producer of Corrèze, ties some similar flies under the name of *Diabolos*. These flies were inherited from his father and their double collars are, to be sure, made from the rare and precious hackle coming from his Limousin cocks.

Mouches Exquises and *Diabolos* are flies of the Corrèze and are probably quite ancient. They are extraordinary flies.

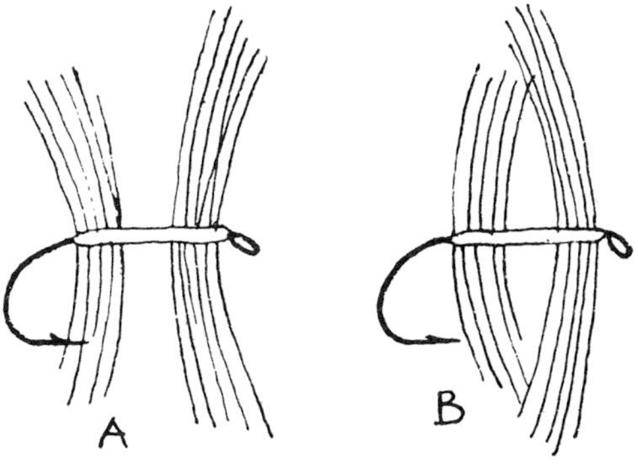

A is preferred to B

Farfelue

Farfelue, in French, means crazy, weird, or irrational. But this little fly of Henry Bresson is capable of regularly seducing the most difficult fish alive—the trout and grayling of the late season of the Doubs at the Moulin du Plain.

The design of the *Farfelue* is that of the classic spider, but in its search for unbelievable color and glitter, it tries to surpass its ancestors of close inspiration, *la Loue* and *la Favorite* of de Chamberet.

Here is the surprising design:

Hook:	18
Tying Thread:	Violet
Tails:	None
Body:	Bright violet tinsel
Hackle:	Four turns of mauve

You can forget everything that has been declared by the imitationists. Do not doubt for a moment that this fly is very effective for trout and grayling.

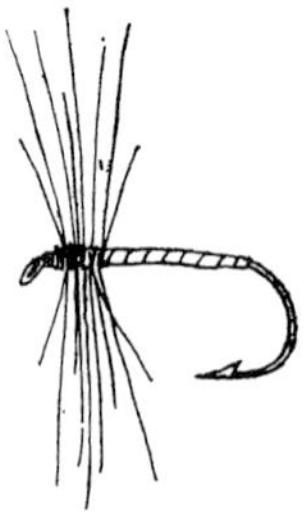

Favorite of Carrère

Ma Favorite was described in 1937 by Louis Carrère in his book, *Mouche Noyée* (The Wet Fly).

Its design is as follows:

Hook:	11 to 13, red tying silk
Tag:	Red wool at the tail
Body:	Black peacock herl
Hackle:	Reddish brown, tied Spanish style

This is certainly a fancy fly and it is almost identical to the English Red Tag, which is used for trout and especially for grayling, as both a wet and dry fly. It is only the method of tying the hackle in the Spanish style that brings something new to the English wet-fly design. Perhaps Carrère did not know of that rather old English fly that dates from around 1850.

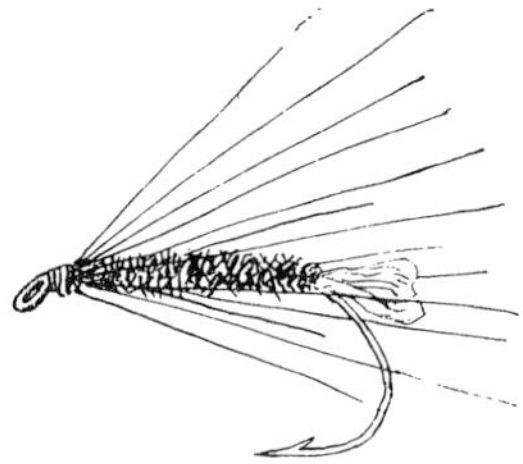

Favorite of de Chamberet

This fly is the second item in the *La Loue* series of flies, dressed by Gérard de Chamberet in the 1930s. It is also called the *Favorite Mauve* or the *Mauve*. Both L. de Boisset, the famous French fishing author, and Charles Ritz found it a very good fly for late-season fishing.

It is dressed as follows:

Hook:	15 or 16
Tails:	Cream
Body:	Brick red quill
Hackle:	Violet-dyed cock

Hackle dyed in rare colors such as rose, mauve, or violet is said to be attractive for grayling even though such colors are not to be found in the world of living insects. Such exotic flies seem to be a specialty of eastern France. They are not found in any English or American series. When the Anglo-Saxons are carried away by fantasy they seem more fascinated by silver and gold tinsel, jungle cock, and golden pheasant tippets.

Favorite of Gallay

Doctor Gallay was a physician of Caen who fished the Touques. Beyond this, nothing is known about the origin of the fly that is still used very much on the Touques and some of its neighboring rivers in Normandy. It is impossible to be very precise about the original dressing due to a total lack of documentation. In its region of origin, the usual design is as follows:

Hook:	14 to 16
Tails:	If tails are desired, they are made of grayish chinchilla hackle fibers
Body:	Almond green wool
Hackle:	Two grayish chinchilla hackles with the shorter wound on the body in palmer style

There are some versions of this fly with wings. Some of these are made with feather wings, often laid forward in the Norman style. Others have cock- or duck-fiber wings. H. Pèthe, in the bulletins of the association Mouches-Salmonidés, described a quite different fly, a spider of the usual form with tails and two badger hackles wound in at the head.

All these flies may be considered as general representations of little mayfly duns. But, for the fisherman of the Touques, it is considered a specific imitation, perhaps of *Baetis*, perhaps of *Ephemerella*. It often happens that they will say, "Today there was a good hatch of *Gallay* . . ."

Gallica

Halford's *Modern Development of the Dry Fly* appeared in 1911. The hundred patterns of imitations set forth in his previous books were reduced to a series of thirty-three dressings said to represent the major part of British insects having interest for fishermen. The collection was the result of long years of research by an angler of genius and experience. It has remained a classic for all those who believe that an artificial fly should be, above all, an imitation of nature.

L. de Boisset (Léonce Vallette), the best French fishing author, was Halfordian in spirit but Gallican in sentiment. He set himself the task of establishing a series equivalent to that of Halford. His research was more exhaustive than that of the English master and he was to include some Ephemeroptera unknown in England, but abundant in France. He was fortunate by being assisted in this imposing effort by two men of exceptional competence who were both remarkable anglers. One, Georges Massia, taught parasitology at the Faculté of Medicine of Lyon and was also very knowledgeable in entomology. The other, Gérard de Chamberet, was a superb dresser of flies who had made a profession of his art.

The *Gallica* series, rich with thirty-seven patterns, was described in 1939 in de Boisset's *Les Mouches du Pêcheur de Truites*. This book is the most important work in French fishing literature. It was republished in 1951 and 1971 and has been studied by all serious French fly fishers. For that reason I have not reproduced here the listing of the thirty-seven patterns and their design. The series, however, does require some comment.

Thirty-five of the thirty-seven dressings are imitative of the Ephemeroptera and only two of Trichoptera. Like many classic fly fishers, de Boisset was primarily interested in the mayflies and consequently gives them the best and, surely, too important part. Different designs are proposed for insects of similar size and appearance. Certain patterns are imitative of insects of really minor distribution, such as the *Leptophlebia* and *Habrophlebia*, or to insects of minor importance to trout here, such as *Polimytarcis virgo*, the manna of slow rivers in which trout and grayling are not predominant. The caddisflies, which are certainly of equal importance to mayflies, are represented by only two patterns and these are unrealistic. Their wings are held away from their bodies, like the English sedge designs. The distinctive characteristic of the most important Trichoptera is the disposition of their parallel wings covering their bodies at rest. This easily imitated feature gives the insect a dense and elongated silhouette that is not found in the *Gallica* imitations.

But above all, there is nothing in the *Gallica* series for the stoneflies, Diptera, and ants. Some stoneflies, the Hawthorn Fly, gnats and smuts, and winged ants are often very important fishing flies. These insects appear in great numbers, trout are avid for them, and they are easy to imitate with simple dressings. It is therefore more profitable to try for a certain resemblance of them than of mayflies.

Despite these faults, the *Gallica* collection is a great and lasting success. It is the only French collection with a deliberate spirit of imitation and its value has never been denied.

I used these beautiful flies for a long time with a preference for those with hackle-fiber wings. Such wings are, in my opinion, unquestionably superior to those made with feather sections. The best were numbers 10, 20, 30, and 31. I recall taking fifty-two trout and two grayling during one afternoon in Germany, almost all of them with a *Gallica* No. 10.

Gamma

The gammarus, or scud, is the little freshwater crustacean that is sometimes called "shrimp." They are very abundant in weed beds or pure and cold waters. Trout are very fond of them. If they are consumed in large numbers they load the flesh of the fish with carotene, which gives it a handsome salmon color.

To be sure, the Americans and English have already created some imitations of this interesting animal. But few, perhaps none, are as realistic as those T. Preskawiec described in Number 44, June 1960, of the *Plaisirs de la Pêche* under the name of *Mouche Gamma*.

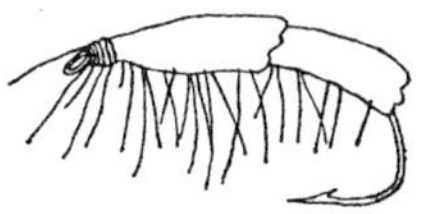

Hook: 11, weighted with fine lead wire

Body: Two grayish beige hackles wound palmer. The body is then covered with two pike scales taken from a fish of three to four pounds. The scales should be dyed beige.

In my opinion, this remarkable artificial is a bit too large. It would be better tied on size 14 to 16 hooks.

Germinal

Gaston Mosrin, of Nantes, fished almost exclusively with wet flies in the Cotentin and Brittany. He created this wet fly and named it after the seventh month of the republican calendar, *Germinal*. This month ran from the middle of March to the middle of April, which happens to be the period when wet flies are most productive on the rivers of Brittany.

Like many of the Breton salmon flies, these trout flies combine stiff and supple hackle—the first is considered to be more lifelike in swift waters and the second in slow currents.

Here is the design:

Hook: 12
Body: Formed of two strips of very fine cotton—one gray, the other light maroon—twisted together. At the rear there is a very light strip of orange wool. The body itself is progressively thinner toward the head
Hackle: Two turns of smokey gray cock hackle mixed with a turn of partridge fibers

The *Germinal* was described by P. Phélipot in *Pêche à la Mouche en Bretagne* (1971).

Gloire de Goumois

(Glory of Goumois)

In this fly pattern, which suggests caddisflies of generally reddish brown tones, I have tried to combine some elements that seem important for sedge designs. While it is necessary to suggest the elongated silhouette of the caddisfly on the water, it is also important to arrive at a good float and to provide good visibility. The use of attractive materials, such as duck or partridge, which are dull and somewhat opaque, is good. But, since they droop a bit when moist, the fibers should be mixed with stiff cock hackle. I have therefore replaced the usual feather-section wing lying back over the body with a cone of mixed cock and partridge fibers. These also do a good job of concealing the hook shank, while at the same time, giving a substantial silhouette and providing for a good float. The desired result can be achieved only by insuring that the cone is evenly distributed around the hook shank with as many fibers below as above.

The design:

Hook:	10 or 12, yellow tying thread
Body:	Tying thread
Wings:	A well-mixed cone of brown partridge and reddish brown cock hackle fibers
Hackle:	A few turns of reddish brown cock hackle supporting one or two turns of brown partridge at the head

The head of the cone, once tied down, should be well soaked with head cement and the hackle wound on and fixed before the cement is completely dry.

A frequent fault of the *Gloire de Goumois* flies I have seen is a poorly integrated dressing with the cone too long and too much to the rear so that the head hackle seems to be separated from the rest of the fly. Such a "semitrailer" effect is far from the desired silhouette—elongated but still compact, as of the caddisfly.

In my opinion, the body, hidden within the cone, is not of great importance. The use of heavy and absorbant material such as wool or fur is to be avoided for true dry flies. If such a body is required, then it is better to tie it by tightly winding a hackle and then trimming it down to the form of the body desired.

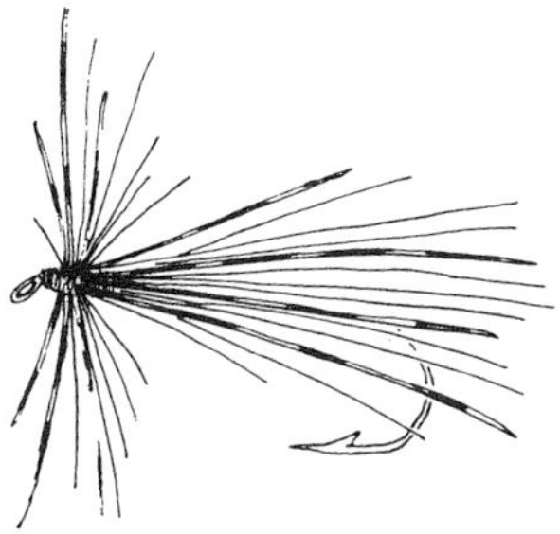

Gloire de Neublans

We are indebted to L. de Boisset and Gérard de Chamberet for this grayling fly that carries the name of a village on the lower Doubs, near Pierre-de-Bresse. Some decades ago this part of the Doubs was very rich in grayling and the best anglers of France met each other there during the late season, October and November.

The fly is a spider with a simple dressing:

Hook:	16 to 18
Tails:	Light, almost white, hackle fibers
Body:	Dark brown tying thread
Hackle:	Light, almost white, cock hackle

De Boisset considered this fly an imitation of *Caenis*. It was one of the preferred grayling flies of Charles Ritz, who made a reputation for it in foreign lands. It is found in English collections and is also known in Bavaria and Austria.

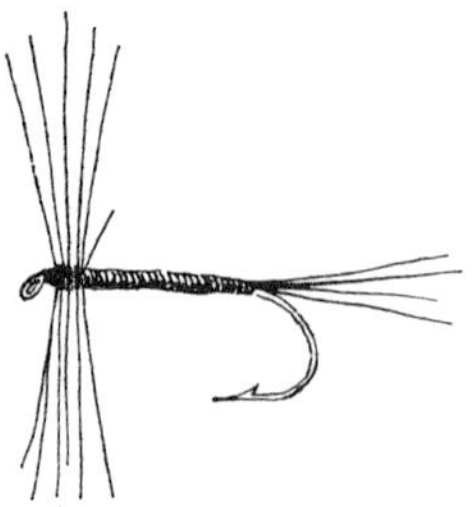

Grise à Corps Jaune

(The Gray with Yellow Body)

This is the typical fly of the provincial market fisherman who wants something simple, solid, and effective. While it is found everywhere in France, it is mostly a fly of the Franche-Comté. The great fishermen of Champagnole, Gabriel Née, Amédée Gros, Maurice Simonet, and Aimé Devaux, have taken tens and even hundreds of thousands of trout with it. And not just any trout, but the trout of the river Ain, which, in public waters, are certainly the most difficult in existence.

The *Grise à Corps Jaune* can be taken for a generalized fly that suggests the Ephemeroptera duns, from the smallest pale olives to the green drake or that uniquely European fly *Oligoneuriella rhenana* when tied in large sizes, passing by the *Ephemerella* and *Heptageniidae.*

It is dressed as follows:

Hook:	10 to 18, yellow tying silk
Tails:	Gray, sometimes reddish brown hackle fibers
Body:	In yellow tying silk. If this thread is lightly waxed and tied with somewhat soiled fingers, it takes on a greenish tint. This is considered the touch of the master by some connoisseurs
Hackle:	Gray, generally solid in color and, if possible, natural. All tones are permitted and all are good

There are numerous variations of this fly. Bodies of floss or raffia, or ribbed, are permitted. However, these are refinements not in the true spirit of this design.

The fly preferred by Amédée Gros has hackles that are trimmed on the bottom to provide an even horizontal support base. The tails are inclined downward to keep the hook point out of the water.

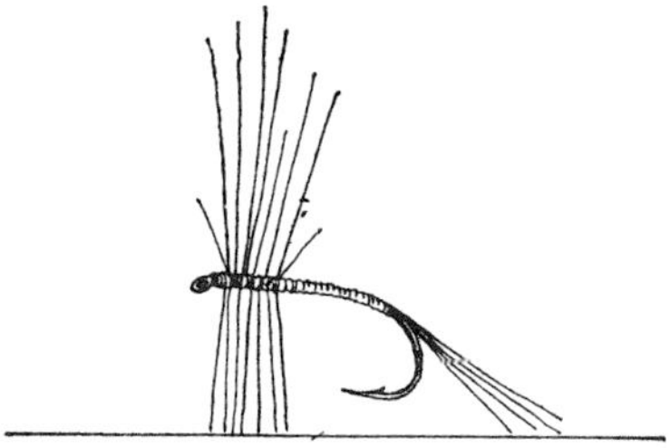

The fly of Simonet had no tail, or if it had one, it was nothing but a suggestion made with the remainder of the hackle stem. The hackle was tied in at the head and wound back toward the bend, the finishing knot at the shoulder of the bend.

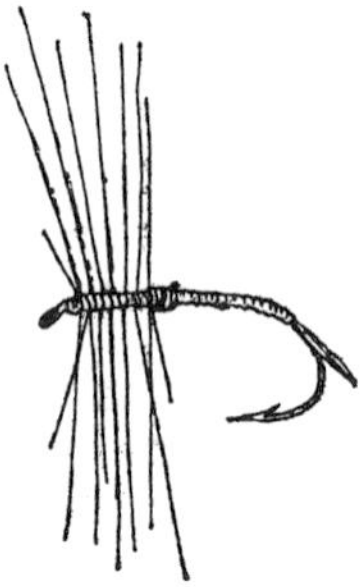

Devaux used two hackles in order to thicken the collar and improve the float. The fibers of the rear hackle are bent forward by the finishing knot made at the shoulder of the shank. This type of dressing, which is found on most of the dry flies of Devaux, is called a "reverse" or "umbrella" dressing. It is designed to prevent the hackle from lying back after use. The tails, tied horizontally, are russet. It is called the "A4" and is the most popular of his collection. Devaux nicknamed it the *Passe-Partout* (pass key) and estimated that it was responsible for eighty percent of the trout he took.

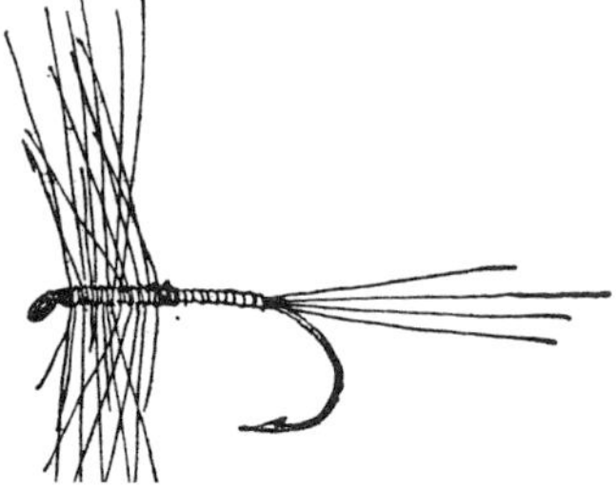

The value of the *Grise à Corps Jaune* depends essentially on the quality of its hackle. Gabriel Née, who had cocks of Spanish origin, put great importance on the use of natural gray hackle. That is the reason why flies of his fabrication were very much in demand.

As a faithful Comtois, I consider this fly superior in effectiveness over all the specific or generic winged imitations of olives, even those that have excellent hackle fiber wings. It holds well on all types of waters, even those of the rivers of Normandy.

I used the classic version, that of Née, for a long time before coming up with a double-collar variation I named *Coquine* and that I now prefer because of its superior float and balance on the water. But I continue to dress and use some spiders of the traditional type when I want to test the exact value of a hackle, and also because I feel a fly of such excellence should not be abandoned.

Incomparable

One thing is certain—with such a name, the creator of this fly cannot be accused of false modesty. To be sure, this is true of Guy Plas, the Correzian hackle raiser whose fishing cocks inspire dreams in all French fly fishermen.

The general structure of the *Incomparable* is classic: it is a tailed spider with a reinforced head hackle, a pattern close to those of the market fishermen of the center of France and of the Jura. But the search for sumptuousness in the choice of materials is here pushed very far. The horizontal tails are in gray spade hackle fibers. Bodies are in red, brown, orange, or yellow olive laquered silk.

It is with the hackle collar that we approach the sublime. This is made by two rare-enough elements that discourage any imitation—at the head a false hackle of the spotted fibers of "pardo" spade hackle and behind that, in support, an ash gray hackle, obviously natural.

Pardos (pardas in the feminine) feathers are produced by some cocks and cannot be perpetuated by breeding—they are rare and precious accidents of nature. They are never neck hackles but are back feathers in the form of spades called cape-spades. For centuries they have been passionately hunted in Spain, in the region of León, to make extremely attractive wet flies. They are attractive because of their spotting, finer but more distinct than those of the partridge, and marvelously evoke the segmented and articulated appendages of insects. We French are forced to ask ourselves how the English and the Americans have continued to live in ignorance of these marvels.

The fibers of the spades are long. To use them in the collar of a dry fly, small or medium, it is necessary to contrive a false collar, a delicate operation even for a professional fly dresser. I admit that my own results have been so poor that I have abandoned this work to someone more skillful. Guy Plas has not dodged the difficulty. The pardo fibers are tied in the desired length, spread into a collar, and then raised. They are tied in with the brilliant side forward, while the ashy gray hackle is wound with the shiny side to the rear. From all directions the trout sees only the pretty things. How can he possibly resist?

Such a fly is evidently quite expensive and those who strike a bit roughly risk regrets. Guy Plas's dressings are as solid as their material is beautiful, so the *Incomparable* permits the taking of a good number of fish before knowing the destiny of all things made by men.

Irrésistible de Cuvelier

This is a rather old Breton pattern that is probably the ancestor of the *Panama*. In effect, the *Panama* did not appear until the twenties and André Ragot remembers that a professional fly tier, Mme. Gourmelon-Cren, of Lambezellec, near Brest, was well known for her models of the *Irrésistibles de Cuvelier* before then. My own research in this area was without positive result. The fly that carries the name of Cuvelier was first described by Léon Tillier in the January 1937 issue of the *Pêche Illustrée*.

The design of the *Irrésistible* is very close to the male variant of the *Panama*.

Hook:	8 to 12, black tying silk
Tails:	Golden pheasant tippets
Body:	Natural raffia with a black peacock butt at the tail
Hackle:	Gray partridge supported by two long furnace cock hackles
Wings:	Two, made from the tips of the hackle used as the collar

The *Irrésistible* differs from the *Panama* only in the position of the wings, which are dressed in the classic manner and not flat. In addition, it has only two wings and not four like the *Panama*. The hackle is not wound palmer along the body although the description given by Tillier had that modification.

In Brittany, the *Cuvelier* is considered a free interpretation of the green drake. It is still made and sold in numerous regions with many fishermen taking it for a simplified and more economical form of the *Panama*.

Jacotte

This purely imaginative pattern, designed to be used as an all-purpose fly, was created around 1952 by a dentist of Nancy, André Jacot, angler of talent and a fishing companion and relative of André Ragot.

Hook:	12 to 16
Tails:	Grizzly hackle fibers
Body:	Black tying thread
Hackle:	Two, mixed smoky gray and cree

A spider that floats well, in the spirit of the *Favorite* of Ragot or the *Jean-Marie*, it is, like the others, an excellent dry fly for all circumstances.

Jean-Marie

The *Jean-Marie* was one of the preferred flies of that excellent angler and dresser of flies of the Jura, Gabriel Née, of Syam, a village in the neighborhood of Champagnole. The pattern was named *Jean-Marie* not in memory of the father of Née as I mistakenly wrote in the first edition of this book, but in honor of Jean-Marie de Saisset, a nephew and godchild of Gabriel Cuénod, a very good friend of Née. Gabriel Cuénod de Chateauvieux, a great Swiss fly fisherman, lived on the banks of the Ain at the Moulin des Chaudières and was described by Tony Burnand in a disrespectful chapter of *Pêches de Partout et d'Ailleurs* entitled, "Le Sauvage des Marmites" (The Savage of the Boilers). This extraordinary personality is associated with the birth of this fly.

The formula of the *Jean-Marie* is given in the book *La Truite et l'Ombre* by Gabriel Née, as follows:

Hook:	13 to 16
Tails:	Reddish brown
Body:	Yellow tying silk
Hackle:	A reddish brown hackle followed by a natural gray hackle

It is therefore a spider close to the celebrated *Grise à Corps Jaune*, and even more, an all purpose fly, resembling at the same time the spinner and the dun. Very visible to the fisherman because of the contrast of its two hackles, and floating well because of the space occupied by the hackles on the hook shank, it is effective on almost all waters and in all seasons. It is a fly of the Jura, a true fly of professional fishermen. Those who love simple, classic, and practical dressings can adopt it without reserve as their basic fly.

Née tied a Green Drake variant of the *Jean-Marie* with a

Some Modern

French Fishing Flies

Selected, collected, or tied
especially for this edition

by

Pierre Affre

Various French flies from different tyers

Assassine (*Pequegnot*)

Altière

Pont Audemer

Pont Audemer Variant (*CDC*)

President Billard

Mouches Exquises (*Dr. Jean Juge*)

Incomparable (*Guy Plas*)

Mouche d'Ornans (*CDC variant*)

Panama (*Ragot*)

Voiler (*CDC*)

Gloire de Neublan (*de Chamberet*)

Danicas with extended body (A *favorite of Charles Ritz*)

Diaphanotères (*Dr. Jean Juge*)

Various Green Drakes (*Sold by Ragot*)

Danica May Fly (CDC)

Devaux Flies (*Different models of flies developed by Aimé Devaux, a good friend of Dr. Pequegnot*)

Grise à Corps Jaune (*Devaux*)

A Large Sedge (*Devaux*)

Professionelle (*Devaux*)

"Mysterious Mystery Flies"
(A *1938 magazine ad*)

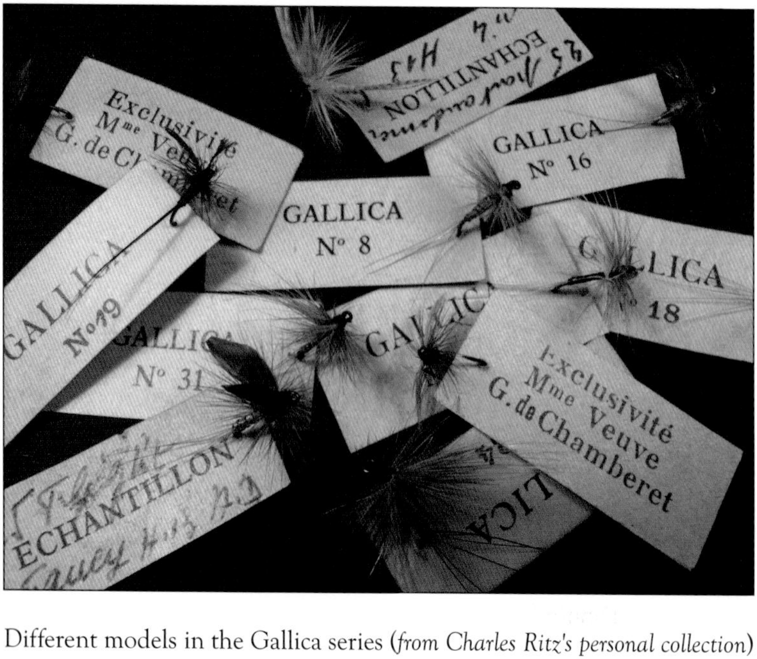

Different models in the Gallica series (*from Charles Ritz's personal collection*)

Bonnenfant (*tied by Lucien Bonnenfant. Wing: a few hairs of badger mixed with donkey*)

Dindin (*invented and tied by Jean-Michel Dubos*)

Some Flies for Salmon

Mouche Bretone (*A Brittany salmon fly with wild-boar dubbing for a wing*)

Lefrançois (*A dry fly for salmon*)

Fly of the Ellé

Typical flies for salmon used in Gave d'Oloron (*on the border of Spain*)

Flies Tied by Yann Le Fèvre

Yann Le Fèvre is one of the most talented modern French tyers. In the last thirty years he has done much to revive the tradition of typical Brittany flies. He helped translate Romilly Fedden's classic *Golden Days* (about a British painter's time in Brittany just prior to World War I) and also rediscovered through Dr. Pequegnot's *Fly Fishing in Brittany* many of the traditional flies from that area, both for trout and salmon. Pierre Affre reports that he has used Le Fèvre's Brittany salmon flies with great success in Scotland, Ireland, Norway, the Kola Peninsula, Quebec, and elsewhere.

Various Mouches Bretones

Yar Griz

Yar Rouz

Mouche Noire d l'Odet

Ruz-du

Preska (*A variant of the Doctor K*)

Yar-du

Orielle de lièvre

Poil de lièvre (*Emerger*)

Phryga Nymphe (*Guy Plas*)

Nymphe Jeannot

Lemarchand

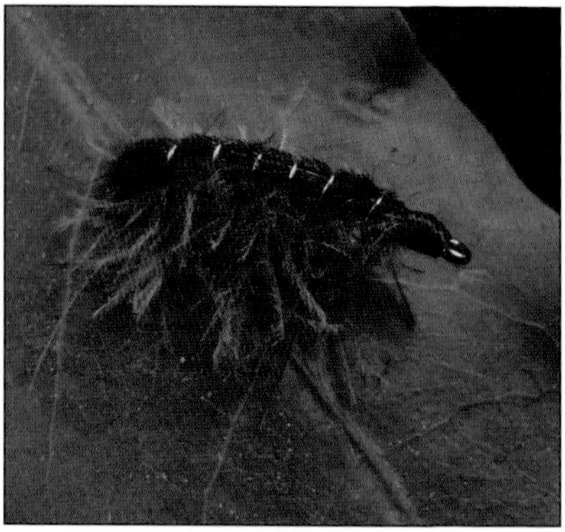

Gamma

Pallaretta

Plumeau (*Ragot*)

Peute (*Henri Bresson*)

Ombrelle (*A brilliant new design by Phillippe Boisson, one of the finest young French fly fishers and innovators*)

Tricolores
(Henri Bresson)

body in varnished raffia ribbed with gold tinsel that I use a great deal, without the gold tinsel, and find it excellent.

The *Jean-Marie* is represented in the Devaux collection by models AK4 and BK4, the latter being of a darker tone. Bresson makes them also in a light gray tone.

It is curious to note that the English, who today tend to simplify and appreciate the practical interest of spiders, use, as a dry fly, a wingless version of the celebrated Greenwell's Glory, said to represent a *Baetis* dun. Courtney Williams, who likes that fly very much, gives the following formula for it:

Hook:	14
Tails:	Furnace cock fibers
Body:	Waxed yellow silk, ribbed with a gold thread
Hackle:	Furnace cock and medium blue-gray cock

This is almost the same thing as the *Jean-Marie* with gold wire and furnace hackle replacing the reddish brown hackle refinements that are perhaps more appreciated by the English angler than by trout.

George Hardy, a fishing journalist of Geneva to whom I owe most of the additional information relating to the history of the *Jean-Marie*, notes that in Geneva there is a similar fly named *Marie-Jeanne*. This feminine version seems to be older than the *Jean-Marie* so it is obviously tempting to establish a relation in one sense or the other. I don't try to resolve that problem, but am content to observe that, whether one style or the other, this generalized fly has an indisputable international vocation.

Nymphe Jeannot

This is a heavily weighted nymph perfected in 1873 by Jean Lysik. He was a fisherman of Brion-sur-Ource who moved to Paris.

Hook: 11 to 13, black tying silk
Tail: Pheasant feather fibers

Abdomen and thorax are formed by windings of medium copper wire that is enameled purple. The abdomen is covered with peacock or heron herl and the wing case is represented on top of the thorax with pheasant or heron fibers. The head should be well formed and varnished. Copper wire windings at the junction of the abdomen and thorax are used to strengthen the dressing material. The copper wire remains bare on the underside of the thorax.

This nymph is designed to be fished deeply and sinks better than the Pheasant Tail and Gray Goose of Sawyer. In addition, it is more durable. It can be found at the store of Dubos, in Paris.

(Drawing—Jean Lysik)

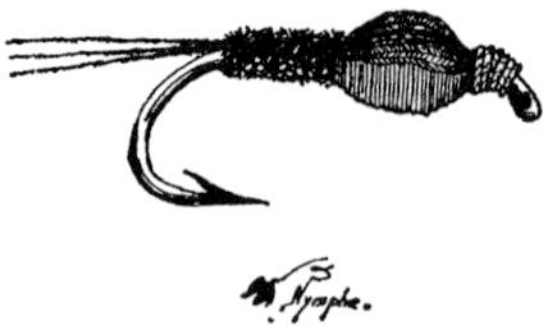

Joliette

The *Joliette* or *Joliette Hopper* is one of the most popular flies of Quebec. It imitates grasshoppers, which are particularly numerous in North America. It is also a general fly, maybe even the unique all-around fly of some anglers of Quebec.

The fly was created in 1945–46 by Bernard Boulard of Joliette, Quebec. Here is its "toilette," as they say in Quebec:

Hook:	6 to 14, black tying thread
Tail:	Red hackle fibers
Body:	Red, orange, or yellow wool ribbed with a russet or ash gray hackle wound palmer
Wings:	Spotted turkey feather sections laid back along the body, lightly spread

The *Joliette* takes with equal ease brown, rainbow, and brook trout. It also takes the "achigans," smallmouth black bass of fresh waters in North America. It can be used greased for dry-fly fishing or ungreased for wet. In large sizes (6 and 8) it also suggests the large stoneflies found on both sides of the Atlantic.

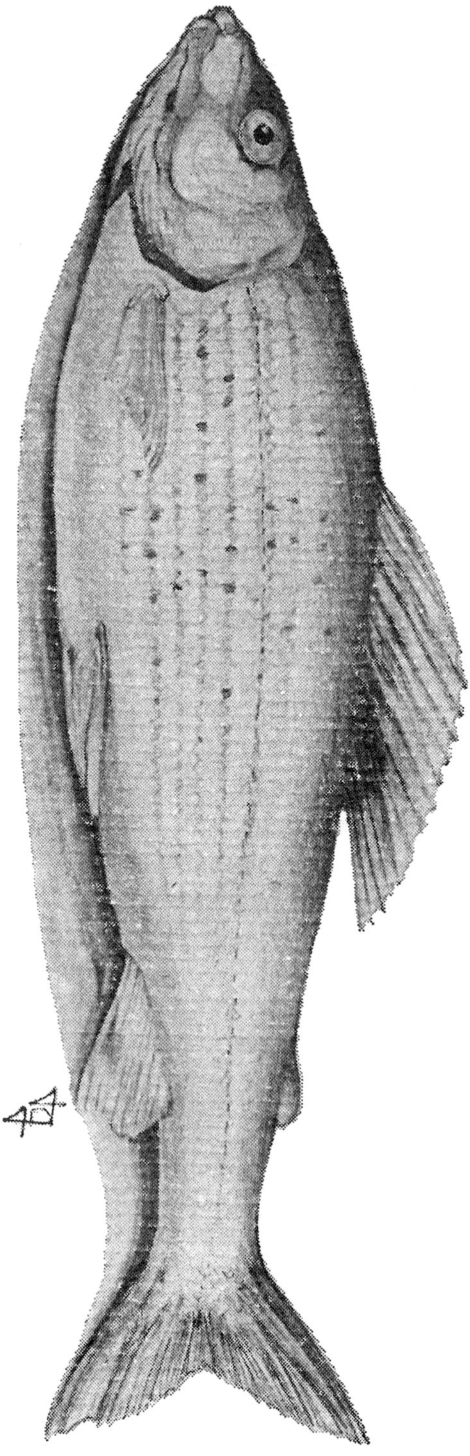

Lefrançois

Americans and Canadians fish for salmon with dry flies that are often large and float well due to their hollow deer-hair bodies. The inventor of this simple and ingenious method of dressing flies has not left his name for posterity so we have no way of knowing if he was a citizen of Canada or the United States. In first place among the recognized patterns in common use is the Bomber. This is a sort of enormous worm with a fusiform body of deer or caribou hair. Bombers are made in all colors, but the brown and white varieties are most favored by salmon fishermen.

The rivers of the Gaspé peninsula in Quebec are of magnificent beauty and absolute clearness. They typify the most perfect kind of dry-fly salmon river. The White Bomber has become extremely popular there and has assumed the agreeable name of a local fisherman of great reputation, Ovila Lefrançois.

Lefrançois was a fishing guide and excellent fly tyer of the Matane river, one of the most productive of the Gaspé peninsula. He was an apostle of the dry fly and took many salmon on his White Bomber. He died prematurely, at the age of 36, and left behind only friends, many regrets, and his name for his favorite fly. Today, as I saw during a trip to the Gaspé, all salmon anglers seem to have several *Lefrançois Speciales* in their fly boxes. And they fish with that fly at least three quarters of the time. The name has become so common and is used in such a widespread manner that a return to the English name of White Bomber does not seem possible.

Here is the design of the *Lefrançois*, not as it was made by the unknown inventor, but by he who modified it slightly and used it so gloriously:

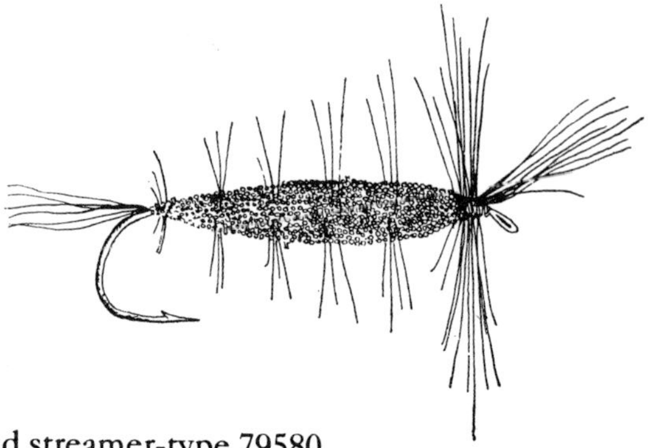

Hook: Mustad streamer-type 79580
Tail: White goat hair or, if not available, calf tail hair
Body: White roebuck or caribou hair, trimmed to a spindle shape and traversed by two badger hackles tied in at the tail by their points and wound up palmer style
Hackle: At the head, two badger hackles and a little wing of the same material as the tail inclined forward at an angle of forty-five degrees

Ovila Lefrançois had a liking for hook size No. 2. This, of course, is an enormous thing that can scarcely be considered a true fly. It is a floating object that defies identification, but that causes the magnificent Gaspésian salmon to rise vigorously. It is cast and recast over the located salmon upstream or across stream. It is as if one were trying to convince a giant grayling that a hatch of *Lefrançois* is underway. And then, if the salmon does not rise, there is an entire bag of gimmicks and tricks that can be used to spark a rise. And, ah, that rise! Those who have lived through it will assure you it is the most awe-inspiring thing in all fly fishing.

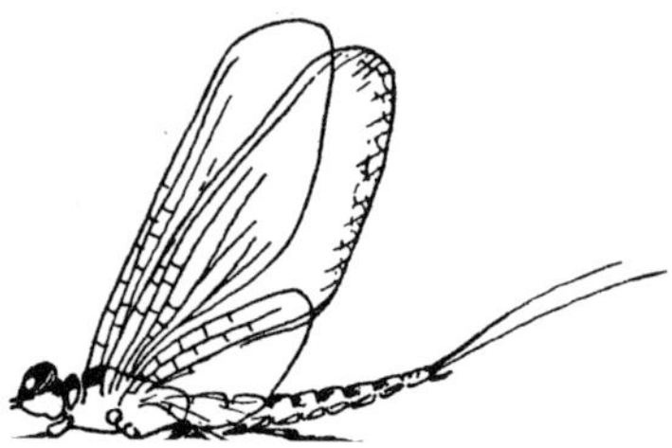

Léhodey

The two brothers Léhodey, quarrymen at l'Abbaye d'Hambye, enjoyed a flattering reputation, around 1935, as great wet-fly fishermen. They fished a Norman river, the Sienne, with a curious wet fly that was rather heavily dressed in palmer-style:

Hook:	9 to 12
Body:	Very light yellow wool
Hackle:	Rose or gray hackle tied in the head and wound palmer back to the bend of the hook

The rose version is more popular than the gray. It is the only rose-colored wet fly that exists, to my knowledge. It is also the only one that uses a palmered dressing. It is currently made by the Ets. Mouches Ragot and is sold in the department of the Manche.

Lemarchand

Known also under the name of D. R. L. (Doctor René Lemarchand of Rouen), this curious wet fly has enjoyed a constant success since its creation, around 1930. Many French fishing authors—Charles Ritz, Tony Burnand, Dr. Barbellion—have spoken of it as a very effective fly. It is sold by most of the fishing-tackle dealers of Paris. It is also known to British authors, such as Lawrie, who gave it an important paragraph in his *Modern Trout Flies*.

According to Henri Pèthe, the original dressing would be that of Colonel Ogareff:

Hook:	Long-shank 11 to 13, sometimes double. Black tying silk
Body:	Black peacock or ostrich: at bend of hook, a few turns of peacock, a few turns of flat silver tinsel to compress the body, then some more turns of peacock, and finally at the front, some turns of flat golden tinsel
Hackle:	Black, laid back along the body

Ogareff thought that the two tinsels, gold and silver, gave the fly a resemblance to a shrimp, a point of view that seems somewhat exaggerated. On current models, the hackle windings are often replaced by a pinch of black or gray hackle fibers tied Spanish-fashion above the hook.

Lièvre et Perdrix

(Hare and Partridge)

This is my favorite nymph. I introduced it in 1971 in the book Pierre Phélipot and I wrote, *Pêche à la Mouche en Bretagne.* It combines the materials I find most water absorbent and attractive to trout: hare's fur, wool, and partridge hackle. I now dress it as follows:

Hook:	12 to 16, fine wire, weighted or unweighted, brown tying silk. If weighted, a foundation of fine copper wire
Tails:	Brown partridge fibers
Abdomen:	Buff yellow wool
Thorax:	Mixed guard and underhair of a hare
Legs:	Imitated by some short fibers of brown partridge at the head and regularly spaced along the sides

I once used bright yellow or olive wool but I now prefer the buff yellow that, once wet, faithfully imitates the color of the ventral face of many nymphs. If a neat and durable dressing is desired, the wool should be unraveled and dubbed in, as is done for hare's fur.

Unweighted, the nymph is fished only a few inches below the surface and is meant for fish that are taking nymphs rising for their transformation into duns. To fish more deeply, the nymph should be weighted. But, in such a case, it must be noted that these patterns sink less well than the hackleless *Poil de Lièvre* of Ragot, or the very sparse patterns of Frank Sawyer.

By lengthening the partridge fibers and suppressing the tails, a wet-fly version results that is good for all fish that take flies. This is good in all sizes.

The drawback of the *Lièvre et Perdrix* is a certain fragility. Wool, fur, and partridge are materials that attract trout but do not resist their teeth very well. Still, they are somewhat more resistant than the pheasant tail feather or goose fibers of the English patterns. It is therefore preferable to keep this nymph for those difficult stretches that do not allow the taking of many fish one after the other. Alas, I am afraid that the majority of our waters are now in that category.

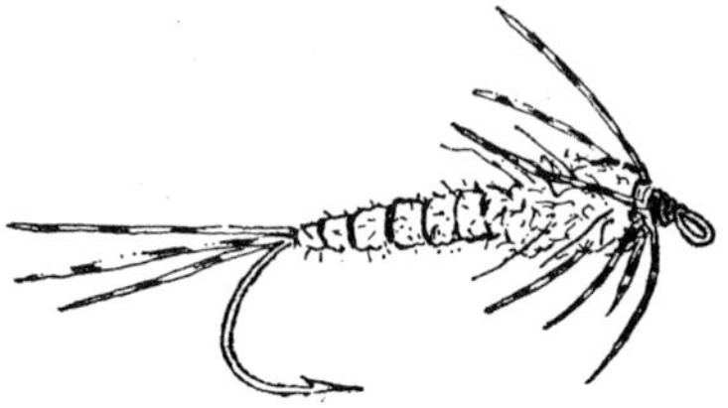

Loge-Coucou

On the Ellé, downstream from Le Faouet, there is a pretty little section on which I have passed some memorable hours in the course of my Breton vacations. This fine place, much reputed and frequented, is located in the neighborhood of a hamlet curiously named *Loge-Coucou* (the cuckoo's cage). I wanted to give this poetic name to a fly I introduced in *Pêche à la Mouche en Bretagne*:

Hook:	16, red tying silk
Tails:	Grizzly hackle fibers
Body:	Very short, in tying silk, covering only the last third of the shank
Hackle:	Two juxtaposed grizzly hackles: one short, covering the middle third of the shank; the other larger, wound on the front third of the shank

The color *coucou*, also called chinchilla gray in France, grizzle or grizzly in Anglo-Saxon literature, is unquestionably attractive because it brings to mind, like partridge, the articulated appendices of insects. It is also very visible to the fisherman. And it is the only natural gray that is easily found commercially. To be sure, the prices are somewhat expensive. A single grizzly neck of good quality costs three or four times as much as common colors.

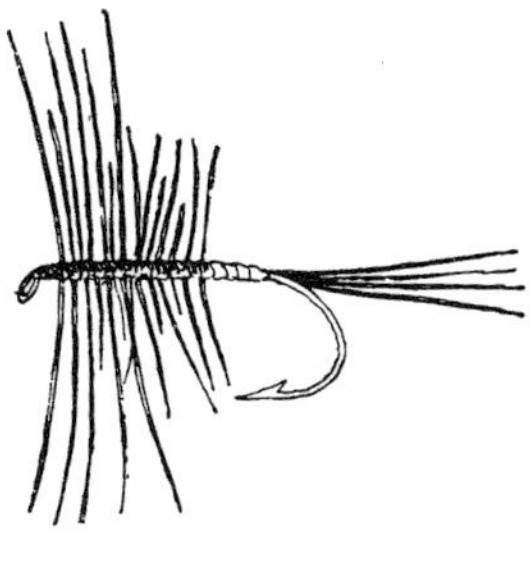

The two hackles are wound rather loosely over the front two-thirds of the hook shank, thereby giving a somewhat better float than the more common dressings that concentrate the hackle at the head.

This is a generalized fly that brings to mind the duns of medium-sized mayflies of the genera *Baetis*, *Ephemerella*, and *Rhithrogena*.

La Loue

La Loue is the first fly of the *La Loue* series, a collection of twelve little grayling flies created by Gérard de Chamberet and described in *Les Mouches du Pêcheur de Truites*, by L. de Boisset.

It is a spider dressed as follows:

Hook:	16 to 18, black tying silk with the finishing knot making a little dark point at the head
Tails:	White hackle fibers
Body:	A quill dyed rose-champagne
Hackle:	Cock hackle dyed rose-champagne

The color of this fly provokes the partisans of imitative or even believable flies because it is certain that no mayfly and probably none of the hundreds of thousands of insect species living on our earth wear clothing of rose-champagne. I believe that there is no fly so completely rose in any English or American collection.

It is striking to note that de Chamberet, who was very much an imitationist in his time, had lively spirits and imaginative taste. In any event, this fly is pretty and takes the grayling of Franche-Comté very well. And, as Paul de Beaulieu, the author of *La Pêche de l'Ombre à la Mouche* points out, the grayling of the Franche-Comté are very difficult to fool. Its advantage is a remarkable visibility—the little rose point it makes on the water remains discernible from a good distance, even in the smaller sizes.

La Loue, often called *La Rose*, continues to be used in Franche-Comté and on the lower Ain river. Charles Ritz, in *Pris sur le Vif* (*A Fly Fisher's Life*), lists it highly among his favorite grayling flies.

Before starting to tie my own flies, I used the *Rose* because of its color, through a certain spirit of contradiction, and to make comparisons. It seems to me that this pattern is neither more nor less effective than any other hackle or similar dressing. And this holds true in all seasons and in all places. Which proves that color . . .

Mademoiselle Rose

I was slow in developing an interest in the traditional wet fly. But I did, finally, in the seventies after having fished for some fifteen years with dry flies and nymphs. Wet-fly fishing seemed to be a kind of angling, which, while agreeable, did not require the same degree of concentration as did the nymph. But it certainly has its place among the techniques used by a complete fly fisherman.

At that time, as an experiment, I made up a series of wet flies using the blackish hair of a silver fox, with bodies of wool in different colors—black, red, yellow, orange, and rose. Curiously enough, the rose seemed to call forth the greatest number of strikes. I was enchanted because the rose fly was pretty and not at all shocking in its natural environment. Soon I was using it almost exclusively. Thus *Mademoiselle Rose* was born and she took quite a few good trout and grayling in France as well as some good rainbows in the Gacka of Yugoslavia.

I developed such confidence in this fly that when I began fishing for salmon in 1976, it was converted into a salmon fly by the simple expedient of making it larger without adding any jungle cock or golden pheasant tippets. I took my fair share of salmon on both sides of the Atlantic and with as much regularity as can be hoped for in that type of fishing. Depending on their luck, some of my friends were successful and swore by *Mademoiselle Rose*; others, less fortunate, as happens with salmon, refused to have any faith in her.

She has brought me sea-run trout, Arctic char, brook trout, and even a lake trout. In October 1984, I planted her in the jaws of some steelhead and numerous coho and Dolly Varden of the Karluk river in Alaska. In that same river in July, my friend Albert Drachkovitch seduced many king salmon with this fly.

The design of *Mademoiselle Rose* is deliberately simple. It is intended to be a light fly, and easy to tie with commonly available materials of practically no cost.

Hook:	All sizes and all types, including double hooks for salmon. Brown or black tying thread
Tail:	Black or blackish hair
Body:	Shrimp rose wool ribbed with tying thread
Throat:	Black or blackish hair
Wing:	Black or blackish hair

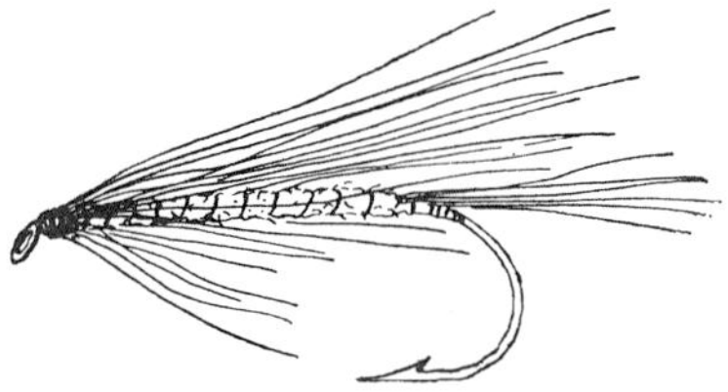

The wool I use is an unraveled pinch of tapestry wool of Colbert, color number 7851. To make the wing, I successively tie in four or five pinches of evenly divided hair, taking care to dress the sides sufficiently. The windings are strengthened by saturation with head cement. I prefer the wing clearly longer than the hook, even for the large salmon models. I also like the tail to be rather long, about half the total length of the hook, and well mounted in the axis of the body—all this to stabilize its swimming in the water.

Any black or blackish hair can be used, but squirrel is particularly good. For the large salmon flies, the incorporation of a pinch of coarse black bear hair provides stiffness. Hair can obviously be replaced by black or dark gray-blue hackle fibers, dyed or natural. For wings of salmon flies larger than No. 6, such substitution is not possible because such long cock hackles do not exist. But all mixtures of feathers and hair are permissible.

To be sure, nymph versions can be made. With them I have taken Arctic char and salmon. And the streamer versions are elegant and good for all fish.

Mistigri

I developed this fly in April 1951 after having examined the stomach contents of several trout taken from the Doubs river at Goumois. I had had the impression that these trout had been feeding on *Baetidae*, but they had taken almost nothing but *Nemouridae*. The *Nemouridae* are widely distributed stoneflies in the Jura at the beginning of spring but there was no established French or English pattern that gave a good suggestion of their little blackish elongated silhouettes. I therefore sought to design a semirepresentative artificial where the wings would be simulated by an out-of-focus cone of hackle fibers. The cone would tend to hide the hook in the same manner that I conceived and perfected, with success, the representation of the large caddisflies. The resulting fly immediately proved to be effective and I described it in *l'Art de la Pêche à la Mouche Sèche* as follows:

Hook:	14, black tying silk
Body:	Bronze peacock fibers
Hackle:	One or two turns of black cock hackle
Wings:	Suggested by a cone of black cock hackle and brown partridge fibers, mixed

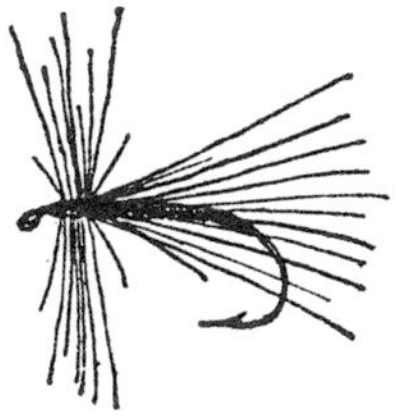

This dressing can be simplified by elimination of the partridge fibers. I have also given up the peacock body and now satisfy myself by covering the hook shank with a layer of black tying thread from front to back, then a second layer, more spaced, coming back toward the hook eye. This dressing is easier for small hooks and, above all, more solid.

While the original design called for only one or two turns of black cock hackle, experience has proven that this is insufficient. At least three turns are required. When natural black hackle is not available, a slate gray one from the Gauloise Bleue breed is just as good.

The important thing about this design is the construction of the cone. It should be full enough to hide the body and shank of the hook so that the point is the only thing that emerges. This can be done by dividing and successively tying in three or four pinches of hackle fibers. The thread should then be tightened so that the fibers are raised to form an angle of twenty to twenty-five degrees with the hook shank.

The base of the formed cone should be soaked with head cement and, while the cement is still fresh, the head hackle wound over the base of the cone. If the hackle is wound in front of the cone base, the fly has a poor appearance, seeming to be made up of separated elements.

The *Mistigri* adequately suggests the nemourids and other blackish little Plecoptera such as the leuctrids and small species of caddisflies that are very much sought after by trout and graylings—*Brachycentrus subnubilis*, the Grannom of the English, for example.

I have used this fly, with success, on varied waters and in different circumstances. Strangely enough, it was on a chalkstream in September when very difficult trout were taking little pale olives that I succeeded best.

In 1978, I chose the *Mistigri* to experiment with, using a single fly for a season. I used it everywhere in France as well as in other countries for an entire year. Only the size of the fly was varied—from 10 to 18. At no time, even during the season of the green drake, did I have any feeling that I might have done better with some other fly.

This rather extensive experiment did, however, bring out the only fault with this fly: it does not float very high on the water and is sometimes difficult to see. This problem can be diminished by replacing the black head hackle with a gray or grizzly one.

I have even used the *Mistigri* as a dry fly for salmon. It is then tied on size 6 to 12 hooks and the body is either the original peacock herl or a trimmed black hackle would palmer to support the great volume of the fly. To it I owe seven salmon—one in Iceland, two in Quebec, and four on Anticosti Island.

Montréal

The *Montréal* is a very old wet fly of Quebec. In fact, it is one of the oldest named flies of North America or elsewhere. Its success has never been denied and it is widely used in Canada and known in the U.S.

Even though it is a fly that could not be more francophone, it was invented in 1840 by an English-speaking man of Scotch origin, Peter Cowan, of Cowansville in Quebec.

It is a vivid fly, with much red, that was originally intended for brook trout (*Salvelinus fontinalis*), the char native to the east of Canada and the U.S. When the brown and rainbow were stocked in Quebec at the end of the past century it proved to be very effective with these fish also. It would surely be as good in Europe.

The easy-to-remember name has contributed as much to its success as its simple dressing:

Tail:	Cock hackle fibers dyed red, or a little section of goose or duck feather dyed red
Body:	Bordeaux or wine-colored silk, ribbed with a fine flat gold tinsel
Hackle:	Dyed bordeaux or wine-colored cock
Wings:	Brown spotted sections of partridge or turkey

The same Peter Cowan also created a *Canada* fly, which differs from the *Montréal* only by a vivid red body and russet throat hackle. It has not acquired the same fame.

There also exists a version of the *Montréal* with a wing of russet squirrel. It is for salmon and has been listed by Fulsher and Krom in *Hair-Wing Atlantic Salmon Flies*. The red tail of the trout fly is replaced by the traditional little lifted tail of golden pheasant, which seems to be a fetish for Atlantic salmon anglers. I question the benefit of this modification. A straight tail, in line with the body, insures the stability of a wet fly and does not detract from its attractiveness. I do not fear missing strikes, especially with salmon.

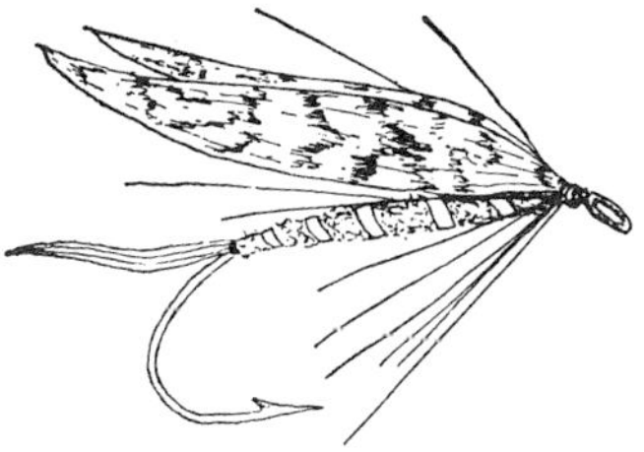

Mouche Noire de l'Odet

(Black Fly of the Odet)

The Odet is the most important of the three little rivers of Quimper, its two sisters being the Steir and the Jet. These are salmon rivers and they were good. They would be good again if they could benefit from a wise and educated management. The Steir and the Jet are today more adapted to fly fishing than the Odet, which has become too obstructed by brush.

A salmon fly that acquired fame in the region of Quimper at the beginning of this century, the *Mouche Noire de l'Odet* is still spoken of, tied, and used by confirmed salmon fishers.

It is a rustic fly, all in black cock hackle:

Hook:	4 to 8
Body:	Black wool. The tail is made up by the tip of a black cock hackle that has been wound palmer over the body
Wings:	Four black cock hackles

In my opinion, two wings would have been sufficient. A body hackle and two wings constitutes the typical Breton salmon fly, which is widely used and simple to make.

Proof has existed for some time that a very brief black fly is one of the best for salmon.

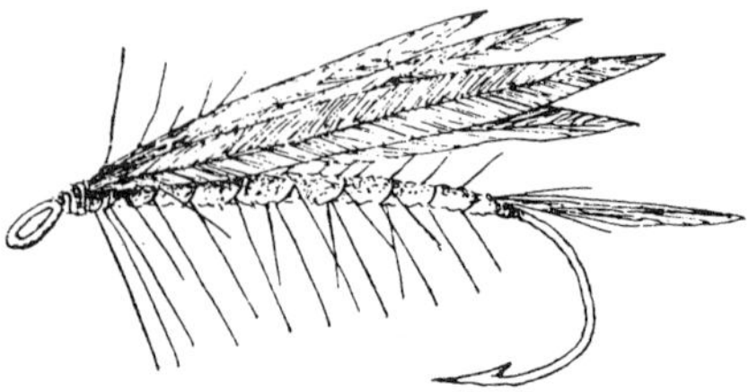

Orange et Faisan

In France, we all know Raymond Rocher as a great specialist in nymph fishing. He had the good fortune to fish the famous Test, where the English say that God himself would have difficulty in getting permission for a day's fishing. It was on this most celebrated chalkstream of England that Rocher perfected a nymph that imitates nothing exactly, but that has proven to be murderous for brown trout and perhaps even better for rainbow trout and grayling.

In English (Rocher is a professor of English), this nymph is Orange and Pheasant. A common enough abbreviation for those who like it is O.P. According to the creator of this fly, it is derived from the Orange and Partridge of Lunn, but it is simpler and, more important, is appreciably weighted:

Hook:	6 to 12, copper wire serving as weight and tying thread
Tail:	Pheasant tail-feather fibers
Body:	Artificial silk floss of bright orange ribbed with gold thread. The back is covered with six to fifteen fibers of pheasant tail feather.

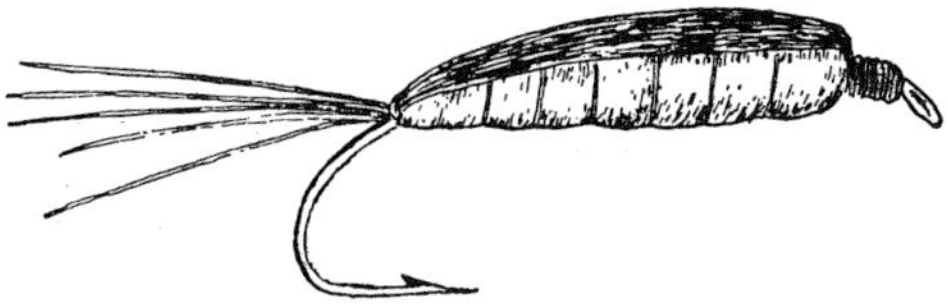

Rocher often elimintates the gold-thread ribbing. Bare of any hackle, the *Orange et Faisan* is a heavy nymph that sinks rapidly and is designed to be fished deeply. Using it requires a long leader. The fly is generally cast upstream with enough slack to allow the heavy larva to sink to the bottom. The line is then tightened and the current allowed to do the work. Even better, an educated animation may be imparted by raising and releasing little wrist movements. All of this depends on the inspiration, experience, and ability—the talent, in short—of the angler.

To be sure, the large nymphs are not pleasant to cast. Their manipulation amuses some and annoys others. But in any case, they permit the taking of large fish that are generally not accessible on other types of flies. They also provide a chance for surprises. Rocher has hooked several salmon in the Test with an *Orange et Faisan*, size 10, and has taken uncountable rudds, roach, and perch, even one of 800 grams. A perch of over a pound and a half on a fly rod would be interesting.

Ornans

These unusual little flies are named after the town of Ornans, capital of the upper Loue river, and birthplace of the painter Courbet.

They have two starling-feather wings that are laid back over the body, and are rather long and pressed against each other. The hackle is short and sparse, grayish or reddish brown in color. Tails are in hackle fiber of the same colors and are somewhat long. The bodies are made of tying silk of many different colors—gray, rose, green, but most frequently yellow.

The design seems somewhat irrational. It falls on its side almost automatically and floats with one of its wings glued to the surface of the water. Such an artificial represents a dun that has collapsed or a spent spinner—one-winged!

The partisans of this fly, numerous on the Loue, make a strong case for it when it comes to fishing for difficult grayling.

These flies of Ornans were undoubtedly created by Gérard de Chamberet and can be found in many of the fishing-tackle stores of Franche-Comté.

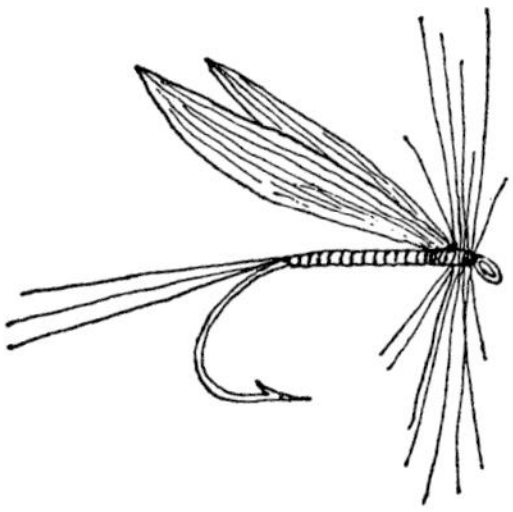

Pallareta

Louis Carrère described this wet fly of Spanish origin in his book, *Mouche Noyée* (1937). He admits that it looks like a larva of the caddisfly, or a maggot.

Hook:	11, wide gape
Tail:	None
Body:	Plump and tapered, in straw yellow silk saturated with several coats of head cement and ribbed with a very fine black silk thread
Hackle:	Bluish gray, tied in on top and laid back Spanish style

Let us pretend that it is more the imitation of the larva of the caddisfly than it is a maggot.

This fly is found almost everywhere in France, but the commercially made ones are almost always, in my opinion, tied on hooks that are too coarse. The hook should have a short shank and a wide gape because the relative thickness of the body reduces the effective gape and can cause missed strikes. At one time there was a great demand in Paris for this fly mounted on double hooks.

The effectiveness of the *Pallareta* is certainly due to its ability to sink more deeply than the usual wet flies. The varnish that covers its voluminous body adds to its weight. Because of this extra weight, it is normally placed at the point when several flies are used on a single cast.

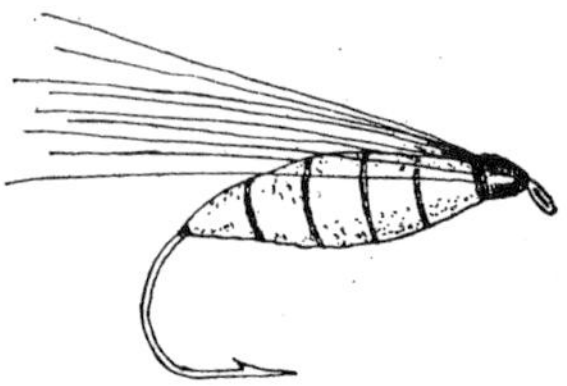

Palm-Ailes

When hackle is wound along the body in palmer or chenille style, the fly floats higher and longer. Wings imitate those of a natural fly, at least to the eyes of the angler, and possibly for the trout as well. Why not associate these two elements? It is probable that this association was common in quite a few rustic flies of the past because such designs are found in certain drawings and woodcuts of ancient flies.

Aimé Devaux told me that he first became interested in this type of fly when he examined some flies from the old mail-order house of Manufrance. He made some, but better dressed, more solid, and with some personal touches. At the time, 1943, he was being hunted by the German occupiers of France and could not make his living in ordinary ways. He lived by fishing—selling or bartering his trout to get by. It makes sense to pay attention to the flies of a man who has to use them to catch fish in order to survive.

Devaux eventually became a professional fly dresser and continued to tie these same flies, giving them the name of *Palm-Ailes* to indicate the association of the *Palm*(er) with *Ailes* (wings). They exist in several versions that differ only in the colors of the hackles used.

Hook:	16 to 18, yellow tying thread
Hackle:	Two or three gray or reddish brown, beginning at the head and occupying the full length of the shank. The tip of the last wind, after being tied off at the bend, is trimmed down to a few millimeters to form a little tail. The tying thread is then brought back to the head by winding between the hackle fibers.
Wings:	Two small hackle points tied down under the finishing knot and bent back "half sedge" style,

> that is, inclined to the rear at about forty-five degrees

The hook size preferred by Devaux was No. 17. Unfortunately, in France the odd sizes of hooks are furnished only to professional dressers and only in very large quantities. I am annoyed by this commercial practice of hookmakers and distributors, and protest in passing.

I think that these flies would be equally excellent in medium and large sizes. They would probably even be good as salmon dry flies. As general-purpose flies, it is difficult to find anything better than these bastard-flies because they vaguely resemble everything that flies over trout streams.

René Sansonnens, who is known to almost everyone who has had the good fortune to fish the river Loue, fishes almost exclusively with this type of fly. He did not copy them from Devaux but reinvented them. Practical minds often have the same ideas.

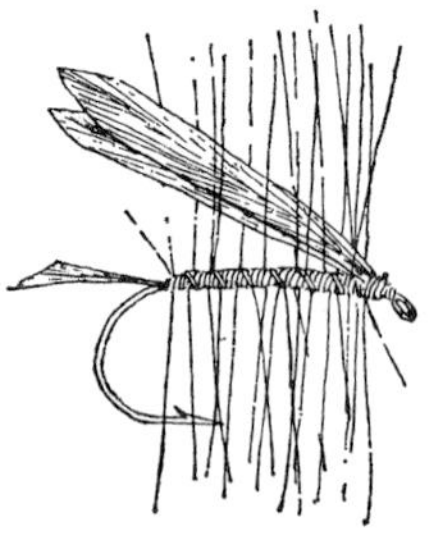

Panama

This fly, of uncertain origin, seems to have come into being between 1920 and 1930. It is first mentioned in a book by Tony Burnand and Charles Ritz, *A la Mouche.* I have never been able to discover who was its father nor learn of the circumstances of its creation. It seems to have been known very early under the name of *Panama du Louvre* at the time Colonel Ogareff was managing the fishing department of the large Parisian store that bore the same name as the famous museum in Paris. The only certainty is that the *Panama* resembles closely a Breton fly, the *Irrésistible de Cuvelier*, which seems to be older.

The *Panama* is richly feathered:

Hook:	8 to 14, black tying silk
Tail:	Tippets from the neck feather of a golden pheasant, orange with black tips
Body:	Natural raffia with four or five ribs of black silk at the tail
Hackle:	One or two reddish brown hackles, depending on the size of the fly. The smallest tied in palmer along the body
Wings:	Four made as follows: two in grizzly hackle tips, tied horizontally in the spent-spinner position; two in dark reddish brown hackle tips, tied in over the others but well separated from them

André Ragot, who was a sly chap, made a female *Panama* that corresponds, more or less, to the above design, and a male *Panama* in which the partridge hackle at the head is darker. Its wings are in furnace hackle points and, at the tail, some windings of peacock herl replace the black silk. I have heard some anglers very seriously comparing the relative merits of the two sexes and it was the female that received the majority of votes.

The *Panama* floats well because of its body hackle and the four wings, which, when correctly dressed, provide very good support. The variety of material used results in a fly that is pleasing to the angler and avoids the impression of a too homogeneous mass. This is a pretty fly and a good one. It is also expensive because of the complexity of the dressing.

It is disliked by imitationists. They see it as a generalized fly suggesting either the green drake or the caddisflies. It must be admitted that the dimensions of this artificial are on the scale of the largest insects. It is never so effective as from the fifteenth of May to the end of June, the period of emergence of the green drake as well as the larger species of caddisflies. In addition, it is the only available commercial pattern of some effectiveness when the big stoneflies come to rivers like the Loue. But since the big stonefly differs as much from a caddis as does a cabbage head from a human one, I prefer to think that the *Panama* is a good example of an imaginative fly suggesting, at the same time, everything and nothing. The creator of this fly came up with a pattern that is often taken without hesitation in the midst of a hatch of green drakes better than an exact imitation of the natural fly, and, sometimes, I think, better than the natural fly itself. It is not unreasonable to suppose that there is some sort of luring effect in most of the good artificial flies, wet or dry.

The virtues of the *Panama* have been recognized by all modern French fishing authors: Tony Burnand, Charles Ritz, P. Barbellion, and even L. de Boisset, the most imitationist of them all. There is scarcely a fisherman in France who does not know of this fly and who does not have a few copies in his fly box. Some use it almost exclusively. All fishing tackle stores keep a good stock, often of each of the models of several different dressers.

Outside of France, the *Panama* is probably the best known French fishing fly. It is currently used in Italy, Spain, Switzerland, and Germany. An Englishman, Arnold Scott, in an article in *Trout and Salmon* that was dedicated to the *Panama*, proposed a variant intended for the large reservoir trout that rise to caddisflies. He kept the hackles and wings of the original, abandoned the tails, replaced the raffia body with one of hare's ear fur ribbed with tinsel, and baptised the result the *Grand Panama*. This new pattern adds the richness of fur and glitter of tinsel to the already rich features of our fly. That, perhaps, is a great deal.

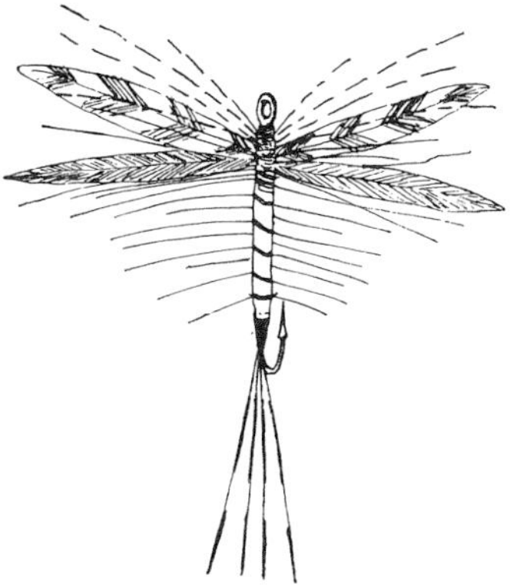

Patate

(Potato)

Among my cousins of Quebec, I have found only a single salmon wet fly of any fame with a French name. And what a name, one of the most prosaic of our language, *la Patate*!

This is also the name of one of the little rivers of Anticosti Island, located in the gulf of the St. Lawrence River, which belonged to Henri Menier at the beginning of this century. He was the king of chocolate, a famous multimillionaire, and undertook to make Anticosti a paradise of hunting and fishing. He succeeded perfectly and the present owner of the island, the Ministère du Loisir, de la Chasse et de la Pêche, continues to develop the work started by the French magnate. Despite its small size, the Patate River produces today up to a hundred small summer salmon.

I know nothing of the manner in which this fly was born on the river of its name, but here is the design:

Hook:	4 to 8
Tail:	None
Body:	Sky blue wool ribbed with a flat silver tinsel
Wing:	White polar bear hair or substitute
Hackle:	Bright yellow cock in a collar placed in the wing after tying
Cheek:	Jungle cock (optional)

The *Patate* is thus a fly of clear tonality and bright colors that really does not bring to mind the vegetable. It is used in Quebec and Newfoundland and is known to some American writers.

Paysanne

(The Country Girl)

In 1931, André Ragot created a series of fully dressed floating spiders that had two mixed wound hackles at the head and a hackle-point tail. The hackles were tied in at the head and wound for a good distance down the shank. The tips of the hackles, which were tied down by a finishing knot at the hook bend, made up the tails. This vigorous caudal appendage was certainly far from a copy of nature but contributed to good balance and gave magnificent flotation.

This series consisted of a large number of patterns that differed from one another in the color of the hackles used. Here are two patterns that are very close to each other, and are distinguished because they enjoy notable reputations:

Ragot No. 4, called the *Favorite of Ragot*

Hook:	11 to 15
Tail:	Two reddish brown and black hackle tips
Body:	Black tying thread
Hackle:	Mixed reddish brown and black

Ragot No. 55bis or *Carhaisienne* (Girl of Carhaix)

The same as the preceding except the hackles are not mixed but tied in one after the other with the black one at the head.

Recently J. L. Pelletier and B. Audouys, in their fly-tying manual, have described the same design under the name of *Paysanne*, a designation I find very well suited to this simple, effective type of dressing. I propose that we all agree to call any hackle-fly design with two or three hackles of which the tips make up the tail *Paysanne.* The variants with reddish brown and black hackles should remain *Favorite of Ragot* and *Carhaisienne* because of their established precedence.

I would like to add that I do believe these flies should be reserved for use on little creeks, over innocent fish. I would like to propose using one of these flies on trout of the Test or the Itchen.

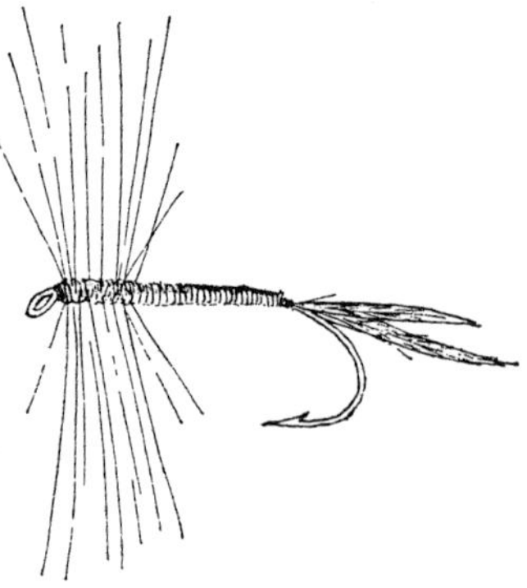

Pébé

Pierre and Patrick Bourret, father and son, are well known fishing-tackle dealers in Lyons. Their initials are the name for a semifancy fly intended for use over the grayling of the lower river of the Ain, grayling that justly excite all Lyonnais.

Hook:	17 to 19
Tail:	Green hackle fibers
Body:	Raw green silk
Hackle:	Green cock hackle
Wings:	Tips of reddish brown hackle tied in flat

Obviously, green is not a color found in the spent spinners of the mayfly, but it is a fact that this fly pleases grayling and trout, as well as the angler.

The success of this fly has caused the Bourrets to develop a yellow-gold variant that has also proven successful. Aimé Devaux produced both the green and yellow *Pébé*.

Peute

Peut (in the feminine, *peute*) is a word of Franc-Comtois dialect that means "ugly." In the *Guerre des Boutons*, Louis Pergaud sometimes puts this word into the mouths of his heroes, and even today it is in common use throughout Franche-Comté and part of Lorraine.

The *Peute*, the most nonconformist of all flies, is the brainchild of Henri Bresson. A gypsy, encountered on the banks of the river Cusancin, passed on to him a deep secret: a feather taken from the breast of a wild female mallard duck has great power during the months of May and June. Bresson designed some rough suggestions of caddisflies with these feathers but the result seemed unpromising, so he did not try them out immediately. Sometime later, he tried them during an evening hatch on the Dessoubre river when the caddisflies were emerging. The result was so spectacular that the fly was immediately baptised and was not long in finding a local audience that has been enlarged continuously since then.

The design is simple:

Hook:	12, 15, or 18
Body:	Yellow tying thread
Hackle:	A female duck feather, with its fibers bent back along the body, held down by the finishing knot

The general hue swings between gray, brown, and cinnamon and its ragged appearance suggests an emerging caddis (see the color plate).

The fly is not a curiosity but a true trout-killer in dry as well as *moist* fly use.

Phryga-Nymphe

The Trichoptera—*phryganes* for the French, *sedges* for the English, and *caddisflies* for the Americans—are aquatic insects that have a complete metamorphosis and go through a pupal stage corresponding to the chrysalis of the butterfly. This stage does not exist for the Ephemeroptera in which the larvae are transformed directly into winged adults. The French entomologists often use the term "nymph" for the pupal stage and it is therefore more justifiable to speak of nymph fishing in connection with the Trichoptera than with the Ephemeroptera.

When the caddisfly pupa comes to maturity, it leaves its case and rises to the surface with the assistance of its long medial legs, which serve as oars. There, it goes through its final metamorphosis to become the perfect insect.

At the beginning of the sixties, Guy Plas perfected a series of five artificials that suggest these emerging insects. They were designed to be fished deeply for the large Yugoslav grayling of the Soca, Unec, Kupa, and Sava rivers. Their originality is in the representation of the long legs of the caddis pupa by spotted pardo cock spade feather fibers.

Hook:	8 to 12, short shank
Body:	Plump. Mixed acrylic fibers in faded colors, light at the rear becoming darker in going forward, ribbed with a dark wire
Collar:	Short and sparse dun spade hackle fibers slanted to the rear with some spotted pardo fibers at the sides and extending beyond the bend of the hook

These flies soon proved to be very killing for trout as well as grayling. Many large fish have fallen to their plump attraction. For some unknown reason they have been nicknamed *Bibis.*

Guy Plas says that if he were forced to use only one type of fly for all the year long, it would be the *Bibi*.

I must confess that my own tastes would incline me more toward one of his gracious dry flies. But it must be admitted that with a *Phryga-Nymphe* or a *Plantureuse* or any other artificial water worm, there are scarcely any days when fish, even many fish, cannot be caught.

Drawing by Ch. Gaidy

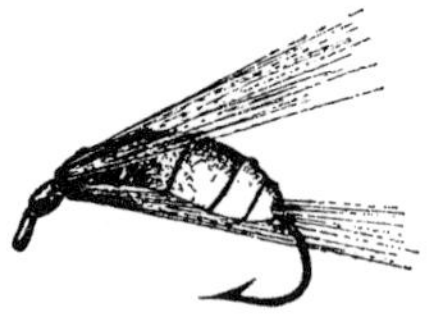

Plantureuse

(Buxom Gal)

The larvae of the caddis and of water worms are among the best natural baits in existence. They are easier to imitate in a realistic manner than are the larvae of the Ephemeroptera, and these imitations have a real attraction for trout and grayling.

I have used for a long time a pattern I call the *Plantureuse* because of its imposing paunch. Following is the current formula:

Hook:	12 to 14, black or dark brown tying silk
Body:	Weighted with copper wire, covered with golden yellow wool, and ribbed with yellow silk to consolidate the wool
Legs:	Suggested by some fibers of brown partridge spread at the head
Head:	Well defined, in dark tying silk

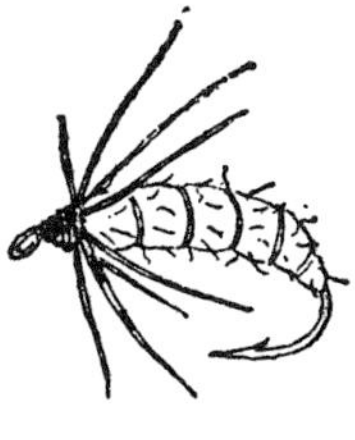

With the help of a mounted needle, the wool can be picked out under the belly of the larva to imitate the ventral gills. This larva is very visible in the water because of its large yellow belly. It can be heavily weighted to bring it down to deep-lying fish. By letting it drift and animating it a bit with small movements of the rod tip . . . but forget that, it is perhaps no longer fly fishing.

Be that as it may, a few of the larva of this type are useful in the box of the angler who wants to overcome a good fish with the aid of a fly rod.

Raymond Rocher fished the Anton, a tributary of the famous Test of England, with his *Ver d'eau Artificiel*. This is almost identical to my *Plantureuse*, but is a yellow salmon color instead of golden yellow. He took a great brown trout of nine pounds with it. Now that is the type of crime I would like to commit.

JEAN-PAUL PEQUEGNOT

Plumeaux

(Feather Dusters)

Both in Normandy and Paris these flies are known as *Plumeaux*—feather dusters. They suggest the green drake (*Ephemera danica*). But here the duck or partridge feather wings of the conventional imitation are replaced by a few turns of the same feathers, supported by one or two turns of cock hackle.

Numerous variations of these flies exist with different colors of feathers and hackle and different material for the bodies and tails. Most commonly, the feather is that of the breast of a mallard duck, dyed yellow, with the supporting hackles reddish brown, and the body in raffia. One of the rare versions that has been defined and given a name, the *Princess de Chimay*, has a bittern hackle and a yellow-wool body. Created on the Varenne, a Norman chalkstream, by Jacqueline de Chimay, it has known its moments of glory.

The *Plumeaux* are in more common use in France than the classic winged imitations of the green drake. They have, in effect, an advantage over the latter because they do not have the twisting effect caused by wings and, despite their rather formless aspect, seem to be more attractive to trout. They are effective in both "moist" and dry fishing.

The most astonishing *Plumeaux* I have seen were on the leaders of the local anglers of the upper Seine, at Vix, a famous place for good trout during the hatch of the green drake. These were giant dry flies dressed on size 6 hooks, or even larger, with tails constructed of entire hackle feathers. These formidable flies, presented on leaders of commensurate size, produced results that were indeed worthy of notice.

Poil de Lièvre

(Hair of the Hare)

Eugène Ragot, father of André, was a druggist in Loudéac and, like many Bretons of fifty years ago, fished only with wet flies. He created the *Poil de Lièvre* around 1910.

Hook:	9 to 12
Body:	Hare's fur with an orange silk tip
Hackle:	Ashy gray or smoky

This excellent wet fly is used throughout Brittany. All of the hare's fur is used, with the guard hairs and underfur mixed, then picked out a little with a needle after the dressing is completed. This gives the body a somewhat ragged appearance that is very lifelike in the water and, without doubt, attracts fish more than the dry and slick bodies made of tying silk or floss.

This attraction was put to good use by André Ragot in 1955 with a nymph version of his father's creation:

Hook:	11 to 15
Tails:	Ash gray cock hackle fibers
Body:	Weighted with a copper wire or not weighted at all; covered at the rear with almond-green wool, and in the front with some dubbed hare fur to represent the thorax
Hackle:	None

I share the opinion of my friend, Yves Rameaux, who believes that this nymph, in its weighted form, is one of the most effective patterns existing anywhere, particularly on chalkstreams.

Pont-Audemer

This celebrated Norman fly is surely derived from the English Mole Fly. Born on the Mole River, in Surrey, the Mole Fly has been completely abandoned on its river of origin, but was adopted in Normandy where it has numerous descendants—the *Pont-Audemer*, *Président Billard*, *Pont l'Evêque*, *Ermenault*, *Grisette*, *Catillon*—and a crowd of others with a temporary or local following.

All these flies have a point in common: their wings are inclined forward at an angle of forty-five degrees over the hackles. The Normans say that these wings are in the form of a hare's ear, but this has nothing to do with the English fly of that name.

The variants of the *Pont-Audemer* are very numerous and it has become difficult to decide which is the original design. For the majority of the Norman anglers, the original had no tails. Such a fly assumes a very unusual posture on the water, the hook penetrating the surface so that the fly is suspended by the hackle collar. The wings are then very visible and the leader forms a little aerial bridge, the value of which is certain and in which I firmly believe.

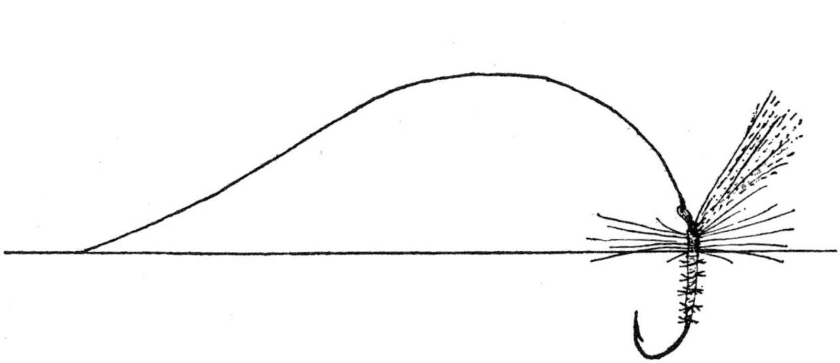

The design can be tied as follows:

Hook:	Medium size, usually 11 to 13, black tying thread
Body:	Natural raffia or yellow silk ribbed by the tying thread or a peacock fiber
Wing:	Mallard flank feathers or bunches of the fibers of these feathers

Variants with tails are frequently found, others have hackle wound palmer-style along the body, as in the Mole Fly, and still others have wings dyed yellow, or are made with white calf's-tail hair. In the latter case, the fly becomes simply a *Queue de Veau* (Calf's Tail), which is very visible and which has its advocates.

In all the versions, the *Pont-Audemer* reminds us mostly of a large mayfly. It is, for all that, clearly smaller than the natural fly, which is perhaps one of the reasons its use is far from being limited to the period of the green drake hatch. It also gives good results when caddisflies emerge. The size is similar. In any event, many of the fishermen of Normandy make the *Pont-Audemer* their basic fly in May and June.

Président Billard

A Norman fly with advanced wings, the *Président Billard* is similar to the *Pont-Audemer*. It can even be considered as the best known variant of the latter.

There is no document or reference that allows fixing its design with precision, and that in itself gives rise to numerous and very different interpretations on the part of tiers. That, to be sure, is the case with most of the flies of Normandy.

Here is the formula of André Ragot:

Hook:	12 to 15
Tails:	Reddish brown
Body:	Yellow wool
Hackle:	Mixed reddish brown and black
Wings:	Turkey

My search has been lengthy, but I do not see what insect this fly is supposed to resemble. It is not the less for that, though. I just hope that those who use it do not consider their fish examples of great selectivity.

Preska

The most characteristic feature of the caddisfly at rest is its silhouette, with elongated wings folded like a roof over the length of the body, covering it almost entirely. Most of the English sedge and many of the French dressings inspired by them do not give sufficient consideration to this major characteristic. It was left to T. Preskawiec to provide an imitation in which the dressing of the wings could be considered realistic, if not exact. In the April-May 1960 issue of *Plaisirs de la Pêche*, this remarkable fly dresser described a general pattern for the large brown caddisflies:

Hook:	11
Body:	Brown eagle or condor quill
Hackle:	Brown cock hackle
Wings:	Brown mallard feathers taken from the breast plate below the white collar, dressed parallel to the hook shank, with the dull concave surfaces facing each other

As the feathers making up the wing are generally too concave, Preskawiec advised correcting them with pressure with the fingernail along the shank.

This murderous fly simply had to carry the diminutive of the name of he who was, with Coloner Ogareff, one of the first and most fecund creators of flies in France. Robert Chino, who knew the father of this fly very well, tells me that Preskawiec started tying these flies in the late forties or very early fifties at the time he was working on rue Paul Cézanne in the shop of Maurice Bousquet, Le Pélican, which was the most stylish fishing-tackle store in France at that time, and was a place through which most of the well known fly fishermen of France and elsewhere passed, including a few Englishmen and Americans. Colonel Milward, General Eisenhower, General Smith, A. J. McClane, Ernest Hemingway, and many others fished at one time or another with flies Preskawiec had tied, including those he called at that time Brown, Black, and Silver Sedge.

Today the Preska Caddisfly is found at most dealers in France. It is probably the best sedge commercially available. It was one of the three or four dry flies in which Charles Ritz placed total confidence.

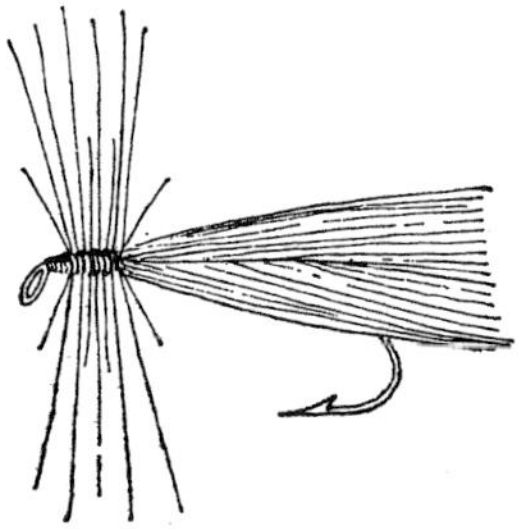

Professionnelle

This is a name that can cause some very strong emotions among the right-thinking personalities of fishing. But are we not all assassins? There is really no reason why we should not examine, without reticence, this compromise of caddis, stonefly, and terrestrial, a product of the practical spirit of Aimé Devaux.

Hook:	13 to 18, brown tying silk
Body:	Tying silk covered with gray or reddish brown hackle, palmered and trimmed
Hackle:	Reddish brown
Wings:	Gray or reddish brown hackle tips, laid back and lightly spread in a V

There are three versions of this fly, three different color combinations. This is an all-purpose fly, to be used during the day as well as during the evening hatch, and from the time of the year when the caddis start to emerge, a time Devaux has said is simultaneous with the appearance of the first leaves.

Note the body to which the trimmed hackle gives volume, without weight or opaqueness. This is a simple and practical idea that should be used in preference to all others when a thick body is desired for a dry fly.

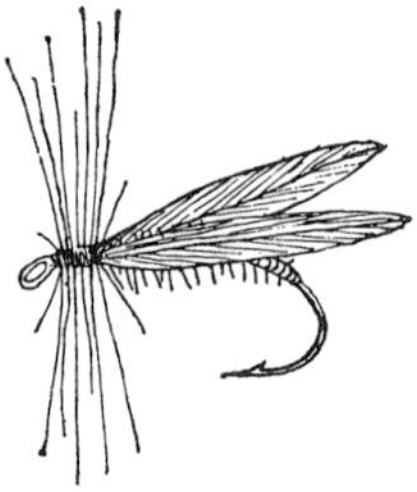

Reine de Cademène

(The Queen of Cademène)

Cademène is a little hamlet located at the center of the best part of the river Loue, the section that runs from Cléron to Chenecey. This part is unsettled and the water is still clean and exceptionally rich in caddisflies. In May and June, an abundant evening hatch of *Odontocerum albicorne*, the silver sedge of the English, results in some really spectacular dusk fishing.

I have tried to suggest this large gray sedge, which so excites trout and grayling, with a dressing similar to that of the *Gloire de Goumois*:

Hook:	10 or 11, yellow tying thread
Body:	Made of the tying thread
Cone:	A mixture of grizzly cock hackle and the spotted gray feather fibers from the breast of a mallard duck
Hackle:	A few turns of grizzly hackle supporting one or two turns of gray partridge

The unkempt aspect obtained is that of the emerging caddis. If made entirely of cock hackle, this semblance disappears; the fly floats better but seems to lose its attraction. If made entirely in duck and partridge, it completely lacks consistency.

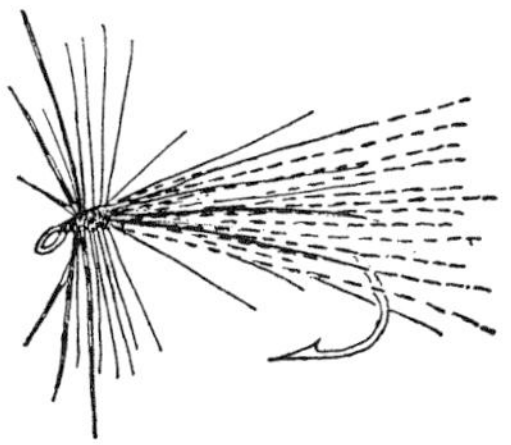

With the *Reine de Cademène*, I have taken hundreds of trout. In the Loue naturally, but also almost everywhere in France, and particularly in Normandy. I use it mostly for the evening fishing in May and June, but also during the day in the presence of emerging large European mayflies. Imitations of the large mayflies twist the leader tippet and easily become sodden. Their large wings and long tails seem to cause numerous missed strikes. I have often noticed that trout taking large mayflies seldom refuse a sedge, so I often find advantage in proposing such a change in diet for the fish.

For those finding the names *Gloire de Goumois* and *Reine de Cademène* pretentious, like the names given to roses in an exhibition or a catalog, I mention that certain of my friends have given a vulgar, but very Franc-Comtois nickname to this fly—*Soufflacul* (blow it up the fanny is a loose translation). After having taken a fish, it is necessary to vigorously blow at the rear of the fly to dry and fluff up the cone. In the calm of the evening this can be heard for some distance and allows easy location of the happy fisherman.

Ruz-Du

A traditional Breton wet fly without wings or tails, this is a personal creation of André Ragot. *Ruz*, in Breton, means red, and *du* means black. This name is very close to the Welsh Coch-y-bondhu, which means red-and-black center. *Coch* also means red in the old Breton language.

That said, the red is usually replaced by orange.

Hook:	10 to 12
Body:	Black tying silk on the front half of the shank with orange at the rear
Hackle:	Black

This rather sparsely dressed fly has proven its utility and is in widespread use in the Finistère. It is found, naturally, in the collection of André Ragot.

Certain Breton salmon fishers use flies that are close to this one, but that are made with black head hackle, black hackle-point wings, and a body with black wool in front and orange at the rear.

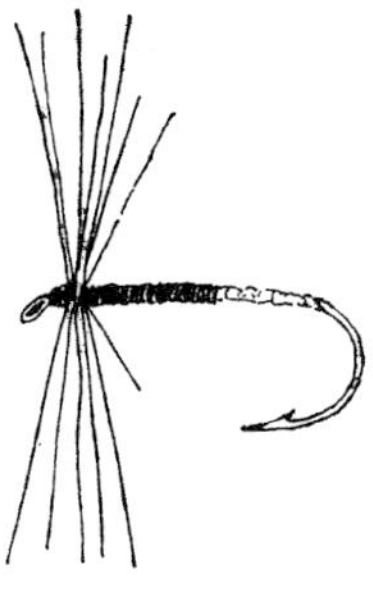

Sub-May

For a French fly, the spelling of *May* would seem to be out of place because May, in French, is *Mai*, and the French are very sensitive about their language. But, as Ronsard has sung to us, "joli mois de may."

T. Preskawiec invented the *Sub-May* as a representation of a mayfly nymph in the process of freeing itself from the nymphal shuck in the surface film—a brief moment of suspension, certainly not more than a few seconds, but a time when the insect is particularly vulnerable and is freely taken by trout. Preskawiec gave the design of his creation in the February-March 1961 issue of the *Plaisirs de la Pêche*:

Hook:	9, long shank
Tails:	None
Abdomen:	Condor quill covered by three pinches of duck fibers dyed greenish yellow. These extend to the rear of the hook by one centimeter at the most and form a sort of sheath simulating the nymphal shuck
Hackle:	Very sparse olive cock

The effectiveness of this fly has been confirmed by numerous modern anglers. But does this mean that the trout actually take this artificial for an emerging mayfly?

I recently recognized the similarity between the *Sub-May* and my *Reine de Cadèmene*. My fly was developed without any knowledge of the fly of Preskawiec and was designed to suggest a large gray sedge. But I have often used my fly when green drakes were on the water. Preskawiec himself, at the end of his description, indicates that in order to make a large silver sedge, it is only necessary to tie the *Sub-May* in gray color.

We know now that a dressing with duck-feather fibers enveloping the body seems to be most effective when there are large mayflies or caddis on the water.

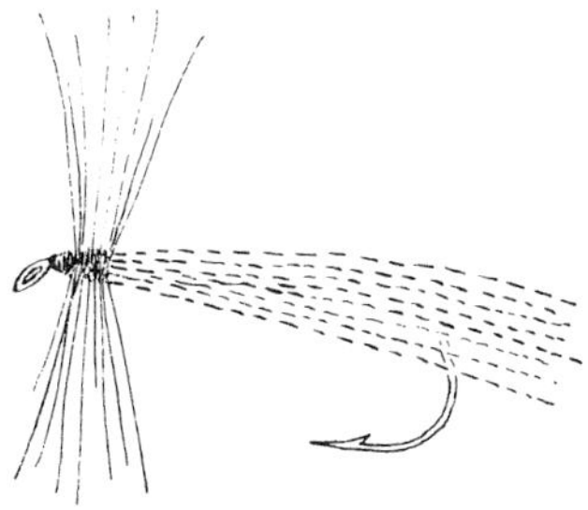

Touyllon

This must be pronounced *Touillon*, but written with a "y", for the correct spelling takes after M. Touyllon, a farmer of Vire, who invented this pretty wet fly around 1910–1920:

Hook:	9 to 12
Tails:	None
Body:	Tip in red silk at the tail, then two or three winds of peacock herl, the front part in yellow silk
Hackle:	Reddish brown

Tricolore

Around 1910, a former tax collector of Guingamp created a very full fly consisting of three different-colored hackles: badger at the head, reddish brown in the middle, light ash gray at the rear. These were wound, one after the other, along almost all of the hook shank. It was almost the reappearance, in a more elaborate form, of the old *Chenille* of Charles de Massas. But, giving in to the taste of modern anglers, it had a little body in black silk, without hackle at that point, and a reddish brown tail.

André Ragot recognized the advantages of this fly which were, to be sure, a good float and visibility superior to that of the classic flies. He gave the fly its present name and added two variants to make up the following trio:

Original Pattern	Tricolore No. 1
Black Hackle at Head	Tricolore No. 2
Yellow Hackle at Head	Tricolore No. 3

The appearance of this almost-palmer on the market was an immense success and millions of copies have left Loudéac for the four corners of the world. It is the French fly that is best known outside of France. Half a dozen dressers tie them all day long for the firm Mouches Ragot.

It can be said that this fly is practically comparable to the Bivisible of Hewitt. The French fly has three colors with the lightest at the back, the American only two with the lighter at the head, but the general idea is the same and the appearance similar. The two flies were created in the same period. When a good idea is in the air, it flies over all the continents.

Universelle

The Belgians are incredibly good at all kinds of fishing—bait, casting, fly, everything. But they are timid in the creation of flies, something that is to be regretted. This is the only widely-known French-language fly I have been able to find in Belgium. It carries the name of *Universelle*, or Universal Sedge or Caddisfly.

It was born around 1930 in the region of Charleroi and its creator was a famous fisherman, Albert Delcourt. After his death in 1935, the fishing tackle dealer Sougné of Brussels started to sell the fly and continues to do so.

The design has tails, which is a common error of that period in models suggesting the Trichoptera:

Hook:	12 to 16
Tails:	Pheasant feather fibers
Body:	Dubbing of hare, ribbed with lemon yellow thread
Wings:	Sections of male or female pheasant wing feather
Hackle:	Reddish brown cock

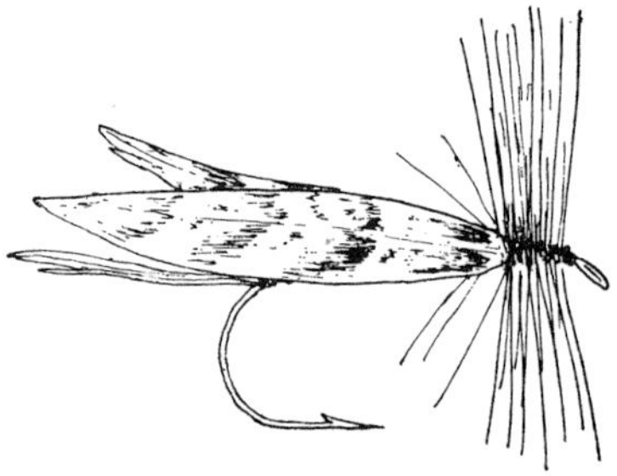

This is a fairly good suggestion of a group of russet sedges and is made and used also in France. The fly is sold under the French name of *Universelle* or the English equivalent of Universal. But I have not found it mentioned in Anglo-Saxon literature nor in the standard works of Barbellion, Burnand, Ritz, or de Boisset.

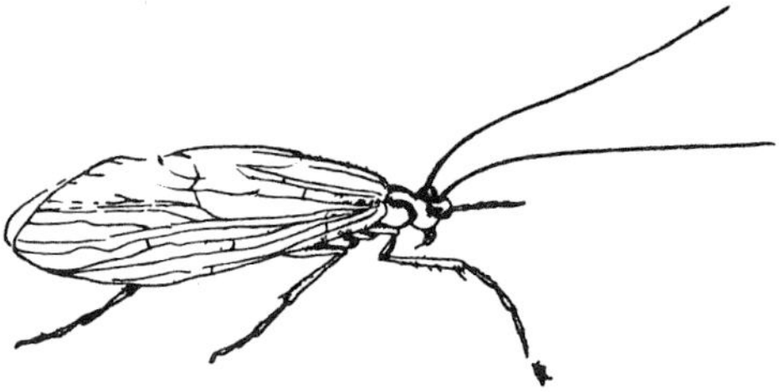

Victoire

Yves Rameaux is a Parisian radiologist and a great angler. Around 1965–1966, on the Andelle River at Perriers, he made some interesting observations and came up with a good idea in fly design. He was perplexed by the fact that, on some days, fish would not rise to artificial flies during abundant hatches of little mayflies. This, despite the presence of numerous rise rings.

By very close observation of the feeding fish through the open planks of a footbridge over the river, he saw that more than half of the duns could not break through the surface film. Some of these insects often managed to push a wing through the surface tension but others, as well as the body of the insect, remained glued in the surface film. Whatever might have been the reason for this inability of the flies to emerge—detergents or some greasy pollutant that increased the surface tension—the trout fed selectively on these trapped insects whether they continued to struggle or had already died from their efforts.

Rameaux developed some flies to represent these insects in their abnormal situation. The immediate success of his efforts, together with the "V" aspect of the flies, resulted in the name of *Victoire*. His intention was to design a fly that floated flush in the surface of the water with no part completely submerged, especially the point and the bend of the hook.

So that the fly would fall with the hook point up, he did away

with the hackle collar and tied in the wings so their tips, as well as the tails, bent toward the point of the hook. The following illustrations give an idea of the aspect of this fly.

Wings and tails are in dark gray cock hackle, the body of red or yellow tying silk.

The *Victoire* is considered by its inventor as a fly, "not *as yet* dry" for fishing *in* the surface film. It requires long and fine leaders, a delicate presentation, and energetic false casts to dry it well.

The upward position of the hook point does not impede hook setting, rather the contrary. It is certain that in keeping the hook point out of the water, the fly is more deceptive.

Viroise

This wet fly comes from the banks of the Vire, a river of the Normandy woodlands. With its badger hackle, its body in black thread at the front and yellow-orange at the tail, it is very similar to the *Ruz-Du*.

X

This abstract little fly was created by Guy Plas, the Limousin fisherman who has a great reputation throughout France for the quality of the fishing cocks he raises.

The fly was described in Number 157 of *Plaisirs de la Pêche*. Tied on No. 18 to 20 hooks, it has two black cock hackle collars that are separated by a little body of black tying thread. This body is limited to the thread required to tie in the hackle points and butts. As can be seen from the illustration, the hook remains bare at the head and above the bend. The two hackles are wound with the shiny sides facing each other so that the natural curve is toward the front for the first hackle and toward the rear for the second. This gives an outline in the form of an "X", which provides the name.

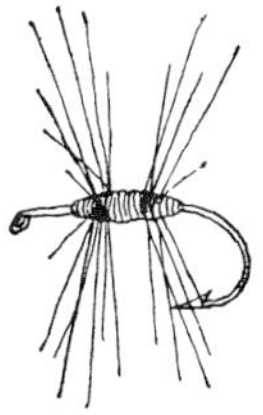

This fly is one of the *Ondines* (Water Sprites), a series of 122 original patterns created by Guy Plas. An important quality of these flies is that their hackles come from the Limousin fishing cocks that Guy Plas breeds and raises with such extraordinary care. This hackle, which is very expensive, has probably never been equaled anywhere else—and I say this with full knowledge of the superb quality of top American necks. A visit to the farm of Guy Plas would be interesting for any fly tier. Each of the selected cocks is treated like a king and each has his private domain. He is allowed to live out his regal life paying only a tribute of some hackles twice a year. No lese majesté here.